DAWSON 01653 £12.39

Equal

IN PRACTICE

D0571421

to be returned on or before
the date stamped below.

3/5

Equal Opportunities
IN PRACTICE

JENNIE LINDON

Hodder & Stoughton

A MEMBER OF THE HODDER HEADLINE GROUP

Orders: please contact Bookpoint Ltd, 130 Milton Park, Abingdon, Oxon OX14 4SB. Telephone: (44) 01235 827720, Fax: (44) 01235 400454. Lines are open from 9.00–6.00, Monday to Saturday, with a 24 hour message answering service. Email address: orders@bookpoint.co.uk

A catalogue record for this title is available from The British Library

ISBN 0 340 705590

First published 1998
Impression number   10 9 8 7 6 5 4
Year   2004 2003 2002

Cover illustration by Gill Sampson

Typeset by Wearset, Boldon, Tyne and Wear.
Printed in Great Britain for Hodder & Stoughton Educational, a division of Hodder Headline Plc, 338 Euston Road, London NW1 3BH by J. W. Arrowsmith Ltd., Bristol.

Dedication

To Drew, Tanith and their friends, from whom I have learned so much about equal opportunities as experienced by children and young people.

Contents

Acknowledgements

Many thanks to my partner, Lance Lindon, who took most of the photographs for this book. I would like to thank the Down's Syndrome Association photo library for the use of the image on page 160. The photograph on page 156 was taken by Patricia George.

I appreciate the involvement of the children, staff and parents of the centres in which many of the photographs were taken: the Balham Nursery School, Balham Family Centre and the Broomwood Methodist Church Parent/Carers and Toddler Group.

I have appreciated so many helpful conversations with Under-Eights Advisors and early years and playworkers that it is impossible to start naming anyone personally. Many of the organisations listed in the book have also been very helpful over the telephone or through their written material. I also continue to learn a great deal from talking with children and young people, who offer a fresh and necessary insight into how equal opportunities in practice is really experienced by the current younger generation.

The examples and case studies in this book have been developed from real people and places, but names and other details have always been changed to maintain confidentiality.

Introduction

This book covers the development of an informed and practical approach to equal opportunities in the different types of early years centres, playwork settings and the first years of primary school. Much of the material will also be helpful if you work with children in a home setting, as a nanny or child minder, or if you are responsible for children in a residential setting.

Chapter 1 provides a discussion of issues that are common to all the areas of equal opportunities: how children learn, the importance of adults' attitudes and the legal framework for good practice. Chapter 2 focuses on equal opportunities in action for girls and boys. Chapter 3 considers how settings can positively approach diversity in ethnic group, cultural tradition and language. Chapter 4 covers how workers can appropriately develop children's understanding of religious belief and practice through activities. Chapter 5 offers information and ideas about working with disabled children and their parents. Finally, Chapter 6 gives an overview of the whole area and some thoughts about the realistic development of good practice.

Each chapter takes a different perspective on the important topic of equal opportunities, but in every case you will find a blend of information, suggestions for activities and encouragement to reflect on your own experience and outlook.

1

Equal opportunities in the early years

How children learn

An active approach to equal opportunities is supported by knowledge of social and historical contexts and concerns about social justice. However, a book that is written for readers who will be responsible for young children must start with the children themselves. An understanding of how children learn has to underpin good practice. Equal opportunities is a real issue for those who work with young children, because they are becoming involved at a time when children are learning about themselves and other people; their attitudes are starting to form.

During early childhood, children are learning an impressive range of skills and a large body of knowledge. By their eighth birthday, they still have a great deal to learn, but they already have a firm view of the world. They have developed, and will continue to develop, their social attitudes about other children and people in general. These attitudes include an outlook on gender, on ethnic and cultural differences and some views about ability and relative disability. Children have developed opinions about and expectations of others, that they judge to be like them, or unlike. Children have also established views, which are still open to change, about their own place in their social world, their personal identity and sense of self-worth.

Awareness of differences

Children are curious; they look at and are interested in people and the events around them. As they learn to talk, children comment out loud on what has caught their interest. What young children say will depend on their experiences so far and therefore will be influenced by their neighbourhood and their own family. Four- and five-year-olds tend to remark on physical differences and contrasts with children or adults who do not fit their experience so far. They notice and often share their observations with familiar adults, assuming that you will be interested as well. Sometimes what children have seen or heard leads them to ask a question, but not always. For instance:

▶ Children may point out an adult who is strikingly tall or heavy in comparison with the adults in their social network. They may comment, 'that lady looks awfully old' or 'why is that man so little?' Part of adults' responsibility is to explain courteously to young children that comments may be accurate, but concern for other people's feelings means that they should be said at less than top volume.

▶ Children are learning about boys and girls and their observation of differences is part of trying to sort out what makes someone a girl or a boy. They may comment about another child, 'Is Nula really a girl? She's got very short hair.'

▶ As children encounter disabled peers or adults, they are likely to comment. For instance, 'Did you know that Andy in my playgroup has a thing to make his ears work?' or, 'Marsha's Daddy sits in a big buggy – why does he do that?'

▶ In a diverse neighbourhood, children may remark that some of their play companions are different in skin colour to themselves. In an area with very little visible ethnic diversity, children may make an accurate observation that seeing a black child or adult is unusual.

CHANGE AND STABILITY

Adults who pay close attention to what children say and to their questions, can learn a great deal about the development of children's thinking, as well as their current knowledge. The observations of parents and carers may be a source of endearing stories about children, but they are also a window onto the world of children.

One area of children's learning focuses on what changes and what does not. Children observe that other people differ in many respects, and they are working out which physical characteristics will change as *they* grow older. Children are initially grounded in the present and what they personally know. So it can be a revelation to a boy that he will not always be a child; one day he will be a man, rather like his father. In a similar way, children are often surprised to realise, perhaps by looking in the family photograph album, that Grandma was once a young person, even a child.

When children realise that some features change, they begin to wonder whether everything can change. They have to learn about those characteristics that are stable throughout life. So, it is not surprising if some children allow for the possibility that their sex or skin colour, or that of their friends, might change as they get older or because of circumstances. Children are learning about health, illness and disability and it is not obvious to them which are the conditions from which people can recover. So a child might reasonably ask, 'When will Andy's ears get better?'

ACTIVITY

Listen to children's comments about the people around them:

▶ **What do they notice and how do they express their interesting observations?**

▶ **What questions do children ask about physical characteristics? About what changes and what stays the same?**

You may explain to a child that comments about people are usually best made in a quieter voice. It is a different situation from calling out, 'Hey, look at the big, yellow digger!', because diggers do not have feelings. Never make children feel badly about being observant. Sometimes it will be appropriate to support children in asking a direct question, so that they avoid talking about other children or adults in their hearing.

THE MEANING OF DIFFERENT

Young children do not automatically assume that *different* means more or less worthy. They are naturally curious and so someone who is 'different' is potentially interesting, merits a comment and sometimes a request for explanation from a parent or carer. Adults, who are only too aware of the prejudices within society, often find it hard to believe that a young child is only commenting, without being aware of a strong social significance.

For instance, after a few weeks in nursery class, my own son (then aged nearly four years) wanted to share his observation about his new friend. Drew asked us, 'Did you know? Matthew is brown, very brown.' The sensible reply was that, yes, we had noticed too. We added that Matthew looked like his parents, and Drew was white because we were white. Drew had no questions arising from his observation, so that was the end of that particular conversation.

From awareness to prejudice

Children who notice physical differences do not immediately assume that some characteristics are more valued. However, they are able to learn negative attitudes with the same ease that they are learning so many other ideas in their young life. Children who observe the prejudiced words or actions of adults or other children, are likely to use what they have experienced to build a negative image of people from a given social or ethnic group, or people with visible disabilities. The development of negative attitudes can limit children's choice of friends, and show in their words and behaviour towards children or adults from the defined group, whom they have learned to value less or to reject.

Children who live in divided communities learn the religious or social distinctions that are important to local adults, even when outsiders would be hard pressed to distinguish between the groups. A generation of children has now grown up with the conflict in Northern Ireland. Early years research and practice has documented the ease with which young Irish children have learned the prejudices and bigotry that support sectarianism, along with the symbols used to tell Catholic apart from Protestant.

Children's personal identity

Young children are developing a sense of themselves as a unique person. Their personal identity is constructed from many aspects:

▶ their own name and an understanding of whether they are a girl or a boy
▶ their immediate family and their place in relation to their parents, brothers and sisters and other close relatives
▶ how they look and how people react to their looks
▶ what they can do and what they cannot do, and whether this seems to matter to other people
▶ their family customs and growing sense of 'what we do in my family'
▶ their experience of cultural tradition and religious belief within everyday life.

Children's sense of identity and their level of self-worth will depend a great deal on their experience of other people – children and adults – and their own social world. Children may feel mainly positive about themselves, that they are worthwhile individuals and valued by others. Or they may doubt themselves and wonder if some of the sources of their personal identity, perhaps being a girl or having a visible disability, make them less valuable than other children.

Positive Pride rather than Superiority

Prejudiced attitudes have an impact on how children feel about themselves, as well as their attitude towards others. Some children learn to boost their sense of self-worth by being disdainful about a child of the opposite sex, rude about a disabled child or rejecting a child from an ethnic group different from their own. Children who have few positive sources of self-esteem, and whose family perhaps experiences a socially deprived position in life, can be especially vulnerable to building an identity through disparaging other social or ethnic groups. Offensive attitudes are not, of course, restricted to those families who have few sources of positive identity. People with no financial worries and a secure social position can be breathtakingly dismissive of others outside their social class or ethnic group.

Children need and deserve a sense of self-esteem, and pride in their own sources of personal identity, but it is unjust if they achieve their own confidence at the cost of other children's self-esteem. Children can learn prejudiced views and a conviction of their own superiority. They are not born feeling and believing that some other people are less worthy than themselves. However, offensive and arrogant attitudes learned by some children will become stronger, unless responsible adults work to counteract the views and any actual misinformation.

ACTIVITY

Over a period of two to three weeks listen in to the names children call each other when they wish to be rude, hurtful or to retaliate. Make a list of the words and divide them into four different types: those that relate to sex differences, to ethnic group, to disability and those words that are general.

Look at the list that you have compiled.

▶ What sort of words are the most common?
▶ Do children seem to understand what they are saying?
▶ Are there some words that children seem more likely to use if they believe that an adult cannot hear?
▶ Are some words that relate to ethnic group or disability used in a more general way?

Positive attitudes in action

Adults can make a difference to how children's attitudes develop but it is important to be realistic about how a positive outlook might work with real children in practice. There has been more discussion within equal opportunities about unacceptable actions and words, than about how children with positive attitudes might behave. Such an imbalance is not surprising when adults are understandably concerned about genuine inequalities within society. However, an emphasis on the current generation has to include serious consideration of the positive things which can happen in groups where children *have* experienced an active approach to equal opportunities.

Children will not always like each other and they will choose to be closer to some friends than to the rest of a group. Children will have disagreements and they will sometimes be rude to one another. Realistically, you cannot hope for a situation in which everybody always gets along or nobody is ever left out of the play. A more sensible goal is that children will relate to one another as individuals, so that friendships develop from shared interests and children can focus on what they have in common, as well as acknowledging that they are not all the same. Your aim is that children are neither chosen nor rejected on the basis of their sex, ethnic group or disabilities.

In a positive early years, playwork or school environment realistic goals might be that:

▶ Friendships and play alliances will sometimes be made between boys and girls, or children of different ethnic groups, when this opportunity is available.
▶ Children will sometimes be angry with each other but they do not resort to insults based on other children's social or ethnic group, their sex or any disability.
▶ Children will be open to changing habits that they bring from elsewhere and some children will actively defend a friend who has been insulted.
▶ Children will learn an open-mindedness about different traditions of dress, diet or language, rather than dismissing a different way as odd or stupid.
▶ Children will learn that positive behaviour applies to everyone. It is no more acceptable for a black child to insult a peer with Down's syndrome than it would be for a white child.
▶ Children can learn to make appropriate allowances for disabled children, but, apart from this sensitivity, they expect their disabled peers to follow the ground rules for the whole group, and that adults should not let children get away with misbehaviour.

ACTIVITY

When you consider equal opportunities, it may seem easier to list the kind of behaviour you do not want from children rather than to focus on what you would like to encourage. The same problem usually arises when teams first try to establish a positive approach to children's general behaviour. It is easier to make a long list of 'what we want to stop'.

Adult good practice will be reflected in relationships between children

▶ Use the section on positive attitudes in action (page 6) to collect observations of children's behaviour, showing that they are developing positive attitudes about being a boy or girl, about their own ethnic group or that of friends, and about disability.
▶ Compare your examples with colleagues or fellow students.
▶ Discuss whether, in your practice, you all tend to focus on unacceptable words and action, rather than building experience of how positive attitudes could develop through children's behaviour.

Adult beliefs about children's attitudes

Some adults are very resistant to considering equal opportunities in early years settings, largely because they discount early childhood as a time when attitudes are formed. This resistance has been reflected in some newspaper stories about this area of good practice. There are a number of assumptions and mistaken beliefs about how young children learn and these are addressed in the following section. You may need to consider some of those points in relation to your own beliefs, or so that you can answer parents' questions.

1   'Children Do Not Notice'

Some adults claim that children are 'innocent' and do not notice social or ethnic group differences, so they cannot develop attitudes based on such visible differences. But how could children not notice and learn? The belief that children are alert to their surroundings and learn from what they hear and see is a fundamental principle in early years work.

2   'To Notice is the Same as Being Prejudiced'

Sometimes, it seems that adults prefer to believe that children do not notice those aspects to the world that adults do not want them to experience. Adults are especially uneasy if they believe that noticing a difference is the same as saying that the difference matters. This would imply that some people are better than others. For instance, many people believe that if you say that children notice ethnic group differences, then you must also be saying that the children are prejudiced – but this is not the case. Adults can no longer easily distinguish awareness and prejudice; children are still learning. A child who notices another child's disability is not automatically being offensive about that child or about disability in general. To notice is not the same as being rude, and adults who tend to jump to this conclusion need to be alert to exactly what children have said and how.

Another source of adults' unease seems to be that they do not know how to react when children express curiosity, voice prejudices about others, or show distress at others' prejudice. It can feel easier to take the approach that alert and curious young children do not notice any of the visible differences of sex, ethnic group or disability.

3   'Children Only Learn What You Deliberately Teach Them'

Adults may claim that, since they never openly acknowledge social or ethnic group differences, they cannot possibly be exerting any influence over children's developing attitudes in this area. This approach is sometimes linked with the claim that children are innocent, and that talking about such topics destroys their innocence.

However convenient these beliefs may be, they are not true. Even limited observation of young children soon shows that they do not just learn what adults intend them to learn, through deliberate telling or showing. Children are also building their attitudes from what they see in their immediate play environment and, by implication, from that which is absent from their books or play materials. They learn from what adults say, and also from the topics of conversation that adults avoid or find uncomfortable.

Some adults believe that, if you avoid a topic, children will learn nothing in that area. But children learn from what is missing from their experience or from the few negative images that adults overlook. For instance, some children live in parts of Britain where the local population is almost entirely white (although it may be diverse in other ways). These children lack the opportunities offered in an ethnically diverse area, of learning through natural contact with real adults and children of different ethnic or cultural origins. So, children in non-diverse areas are very dependent on the quality of books and play materials and the willingness of workers and parents to show them the world beyond their local boundaries.

Even if these adults avoid their responsibilities, it is not the case that the children will learn nothing about ethnic group and remain innocent. On the contrary, white children from largely white localities will develop attitudes based on what remains to fill the gap left by lack of experience or knowledge. These children's only experience of black people, for example, may be through television. The images that they form may be that black people mainly do sporting activities or are at the hub of inner city troubles.

4   'YOU SHOULD TREAT ALL CHILDREN THE SAME'

Some adults will claim that they do not notice any differences between the children for whom they are responsible, that they treat them all the same. This fairly common belief muddles up fair treatment of young children with a refusal to recognise individuality. Children are not all the same and adults have a serious problem if they genuinely do not notice the differences that make children into unique individuals. For instance:

▶ An insistence on treating boys and girls the same can block good professional practice in addressing unspoken assumptions that workers have learned in their own childhood. Girls and boys are not all the same and equal opportunities in practice needs to work out what is an appropriate recognition of difference and what can restrict children's options.

▶ When white early years workers express this belief about ethnic group differences between the children, it almost certainly means that the adults treat all the children as if they are white. Important sources of personal identity for some children are pushed to one side, because adults do not wish to acknowledge the individuality that grows from a positive outlook on ethnic group origins or culture. This approach is sometimes called a colour blind policy.

▶ In a similar way, all disabled children are not the same as non-disabled children. They are children first and foremost and should be treated as such, but their individual disability will shape their experience, in one way or another.

5   'CHILDREN'S ATTITUDES ARE NOT OUR BUSINESS'

Sometimes a staff team, or some members of a group, argue that they should not try to influence children's attitudes over gender or ethnic group and culture, because that would be interfering, perhaps even brainwashing. Yet, many workers are concerned to guide children towards sharing with other children, turn-taking and particular patterns of behaviour at mealtimes. The arguments in favour of these behaviours are expressed in terms of unselfishness, consideration and politeness – in fact, a strongly argued set of attitudes towards other people. Work with young children is not value-free; adults' behaviour is powerfully shaped by what they believe to be important and valuable. Dealing with equal opportunities certainly does not mean imposing values onto a setting which previously had no values at all.

Sooner rather than later, young children will notice social and ethnic group differences, the pattern of differences associated with gender and will become aware of disability. These visible differences will develop meaning, positive or negative, depending entirely on the attitudes that are communicated to children through what is said by adults or by other children, and through the messages that reach them via the play environment. Adults responsible for young children need to be as actively involved in promoting positive social attitudes as they often are about shaping other forms of behaviour.

ACTIVITY

Be honest with yourself and about your own staff team. Do you tend to make any of the comments highlighted in this section? If you are a student, have you heard similar comments expressed to shut down a discussion about equal opportunities?

Try taking one or two comments and ask yourself, or discuss with someone else:

▶ What does this comment actually mean?
▶ Do we really put such sentiments into practice and what would happen if we did?

▶ In what ways are we possibly blocking children's experience or affecting their self-esteem?

Adults' attitudes and behaviour

All adults have developed attitudes about other people and the groups to which they belong. Attitudes are partly made up of feelings about other people or whole groups. But there is also an intellectual part that is formed by beliefs, expectations and assumptions. These are supported by information and the conviction that particular facts are true ('everyone knows that . . .'). You cannot see people's attitudes, but they emerge through behaviour: their actions and their words.

Everyone holds attitudes: some are mainly positive, some may be mildly rejecting of others, but some may be intensely offensive towards particular groups, defined by gender, social class, ethnic group or disability. Attitudes are learned (see the previous section about children) and, although some people may be very fixed in their outlook, adults are capable of continuing to learn and to re-think some of their views and assumptions about others.

TO THINK ABOUT

There is often no neat and easy logic to people's attitudes. Adults who are on the receiving end of offensive behaviour, may in their turn hold negative attitudes about people from other ethnic or social groups, and not feel that their outlook is in any way illogical. Through constructive workshops on attitudes and behaviour, it is possible to develop empathy between individuals who have experienced inequalities or discriminatory behaviour for very different reasons.

Stereotypes

Firm attitudes about groups of people are supported by **stereotypes**: simple, relatively fixed, beliefs about the characteristics shared by individuals of an identified group.

▶ Stereotypes are usually unfavourable, for instance: 'women are always so emotional', 'Muslims are fanatics about their religion' or 'he's so irresponsible – typical working class'.

▶ Apparently complimentary stereotypes can have a serious sting in the tail. They restrict individuals' options to those which fit the stereotype, for instance: 'disabled people are so brave' or 'black boys are natural athletes'.

▶ Stereotypes are usually applied to groups to which the individuals holding the belief do not themselves belong. The process of developing and maintaining a stereotype depends on a belief that other groups have less variety than one's own. People are more ready to say of another social or ethnic group 'they're all . . .' or 'she's a typical . . .'. But they will say of their own group that 'it all depends' or 'people differ, you can't say that about everybody'.

▶ Stereotypes are often built from a particular event or experience, which is then generalised well beyond the original context. Firmly held stereotypes then shape the interpretation placed on other experiences. People who appear to fit the stereotype are taken as further evidence of the truth of the belief. Experience of individuals who clearly do not fit are dismissed as any reason to adjust beliefs because, 'you're my friend, I don't count you', 'he's the exception that proves the rule' or 'most of them aren't like her'.

▶ Stereotypes may be learned during childhood because children hear familiar adults, in the family or outside, expressing simplistic, fixed views about other people. Children remember these beliefs along with other information that they have gained from key adults in their lives. They repeat the beliefs until some experience leads them to question the view.

FOR EXAMPLE:

Stereotypical assumptions do not have to be extremely racist or sexist to offend and annoy those on the receiving end. In a book review for *The Times* in May 1997, Diane Abbott MP recalled her experience.

'I remember going to a Cambridge May Ball as an undergraduate. I was dressed in a long evening dress and made up and be-jewelled to within an inch of my life. Yet, as soon as I came in through the gate someone rushed up to me and said, "Oh, good, you must have come to do the washing up". He did not ask himself why I would wear an evening dress and diamante to do so. He only knew that I was a black woman and therefore must belong in the kitchen.'

Referring to ideas from Patricia Williams' book *Seeing a Colour Blind Future* (Virago, 1997), Diane Abbott described the experience as an example of the 'small aggressions of unconscious racism' rather than an instance of extreme bigotry.

> Whatever your own social or ethnic group, you may have personal examples of when unthinking assumptions from others took you by surprise.

ACTIVITY

Stereotypes link with assumptions about other people and everyone has some working assumptions about life and other people. Sometimes the consequences of these assumptions may not be too serious. But, on other occasions, stereotypical beliefs might support offensive behaviour or have the consequence that people do not receive the support that they need.

Look at the examples that follow.

▶ **What kind of beliefs are the speakers expressing?**
▶ **What seems to be the source of their convictions?**
▶ **What might be the consequences if these views go unchallenged?**

1 'There's no point in asking May's Grandma to help the children on the nursery computer. Older people aren't computer literate and she'll get all worried if we ask her.'
2 'Sally is a typical, worrying first-time mum. They think their babies have got everything from scarlet fever to in-growing toe nails. I tell them not to worry so much and come back in a week.'
3 'We let the boys run around and burn off their energy. There's no point in trying to make them sit at the tables, they only fidget all the time.'
4 'Nur's parents shouldn't be trying to teach the child two languages at the same time. She should be learning English like everyone else. Nur can learn Turkish when she gets older and she's ready.'
5 'Sunita looks a bit tired with the new baby, but she'll be fine. Asians always have these big extended families, don't they? There'll be loads of aunties helping out.'
6 'I'll wait until Liam's mother comes in tomorrow. His father has this dreadful stammer and any conversation takes for ever. It's so embarrassing and I don't think he understands half of what I say.'
7 'We'd better not ask Rebecca's father to help with the Hanukkah celebrations. Jewish people are so touchy, aren't they? I'll never forget Jacob's mother two years ago. I'm not asking any of them again.'
8 'I give the children a proper balanced diet here, none of this vegetarian nonsense. Adults shouldn't impose their wishes on children. They should have a normal diet when they're little, then they can choose for themselves when they get older.'

9 'I think parents of disabled children are over-protective because they feel guilty. I worked with two families and they were always going on about why had it happened to their child and perhaps there was something they could have done.'

10 'We've got some city children visiting us next week. Poor little souls, I expect none of them has ever seen a cow before, let alone walked up a hill. These inner-city families never take their children anywhere.'

11 'We're trying an experiment with ethnic food. You know, trying the children with a mild curry or some kebabs. It's fun but, of course, they don't like it. We make sure there's some ordinary food as well.'

Good practice in equal opportunities

Good practice has several equally important strands:

▶ Good practice is partly a focus on the individual children and families who are currently attending your setting. So your work naturally reflects your immediate environment.

▶ But good practice in equal opportunities also covers the image of the world that you are giving children, the big picture that extends beyond their own backyard.

▶ There is also a moral dimension, that adults are responsible for what children are learning in their setting.

There have been some serious misunderstandings about equal opportunities, some of which have been promoted by the news media.

▶ Equal opportunity does not mean blaming people for the past. A positive approach looks to the future. People cannot be responsible for what happened before they were even born. However, everyone is responsible for their own attitudes now and their willingness, or unwillingness to learn more and to reflect on their views.

▶ Children especially should not be expected to make up for inequalities that have or still do exist. They are not responsible for the society into which they were born. But they can learn about the impact now of their own words and actions and learn a more open approach than was possible for previous generations.

▶ Equal opportunity means everyone is grounded in children's experience now. Black children cannot be excused from offensive remarks to another child. Girls need to show consideration to boys as well as vice versa. Disabled children deserve to be treated as children first, and this brings them responsibilities as well as rights.

▶ Putting equal opportunities into practice is not a competitive exercise

– celebrating Divali does not necessitate 'banning Christmas' (as claimed by a misleading newspaper story some years ago). Children can learn about cultures or religions other than their own and develop a sense of respect.

Language and attitudes

Attitudes are reflected in people's choice of words and phrases, even when they are not conscious of the implications of what they say. Words matter because they are a reflection of deeply entrenched attitudes in our society. For instance:

▶ There are more negative associations with 'black' than 'white'. People talk of 'blackening someone's reputation', of a 'black day', 'blackmail' and there is the weird phrase 'black comedy'. Yet something pure and clean is described as 'whiter than white'.

▶ People who avoid racist remarks based directly on skin colour still sometimes use, perhaps without thinking, other offensive phrases like 'dirty little Arab', 'acting Jewish' (an implication of meanness) or 'welshing on a deal' (going back on an arrangement).

▶ A range of insults are based on a negative view of being female: 'fussing like an old woman' or upset boys being criticised for 'acting just like a girl'. You will still find spoken and written examples when a generic 'he' is used to cover both sexes, or terms like 'man' and 'mankind' when the discussion is about everyone.

▶ Words like 'cripple' or 'spastic' are sometimes used as general insults. Rhetorical questions like 'Are you deaf?' or 'You blind or something?' are used to criticise someone for their inattention.

▶ Unquestioned habits of language also extend to beliefs about those groups about which it is fine to make jokes. In Britain there has been a tradition of 'Irish jokes', in which the punch line depends on a belief that Irish people are stupid. Similar patterns can be found in other countries, except that the ethnic group targeted is different. In the United States this kind of joke is a 'Polish joke' and in Scandinavia it is a 'Norwegian joke'.

TO THINK ABOUT

Previous generations in Britain expressed a casual anti-semitism and disdain of foreigners, and the language became part of ordinary conversation. For instance, if you read some of the Agatha Christie books written in the 1920s or 1930s, you will realise that the heroes and heroines – not the villains – of the story use what we would regard now as offensive language about Jews and dismissive terms for anyone who is not British.

The attitudes about foreigners and black ethnic groups affected books written for children. The views were also very clear in children's comics well up to the 1960s and early 1970s. Comics may not be seen as real literature by adults but children read them with great enthusiasm.

Of course, changing the words people use does not magically change their attitudes. However, an awareness of your use of words is a valuable part of a more general willingness to consider your attitudes.

A POSITIVE APPROACH TO LANGUAGE

Every staff team needs to have a constructive approach to language. Nagging people or only highlighting what they say that is wrong can seriously undermine staff morale. The negative consequence is then that workers become much more concerned about what they are not allowed to say than in considering the views that underlie the words. Heads of centres and senior workers need to encourage colleagues to stand back from the assumptions shown by their use of language. Many people will need to change habits that have been established when they were still young and not in the position to make an informed decision.

Some positive guidelines include:

▶ Avoid simple criticisms of 'you shouldn't say that' or 'that's such a racist thing to say'. It is unhelpful to label a colleague as 'sexist' or 'anti-semitic'. Labels leave people with no room to manoeuvre and push them towards a defensive reply, rather than encouraging them to think about their views. Nor do you want the children to learn to deal with each other mainly through blunt accusations.

▶ Be prepared to explain why you find something offensive, or the reason you believe a phrase is unacceptable in your setting. Move towards honest comments such as, 'I find it hard to hear you describe Sunita as "gabbling away in her own language". Do we gabble then?'

▶ A more general discussion in a team could be about food from other cultures. What does it say about our views that we talk about 'ethnic food'? Why isn't fish and chips 'ethnic food'? On the subject of religion, you might want to think about what it means to say if someone says, 'Oh, that family is just normal C of E'.

▶ Focus on what you would like workers to say and not just on what they should not say, or do. For instance, you might want a group of workers to stop making sweeping generalisations like 'girls are far more helpful than boys'. But these workers will probably need some practical guidance beyond 'please stop saying that'. They may need to focus on individual children and their helpful behaviour. The workers may also need to look at their own actions: whom do they ask to help and in what way? Observation of both children and workers might help to change beliefs and practice.

A useful parallel is to remember the elements of a positive approach to children's behaviour and to examine colleagues' words and actions with a similar constructive outlook.

Focus on the children

You can make a difference to young children's attitudes but, of course, you have to remain realistic about what you can and cannot do. Early years and playwork settings cannot take up the burden of righting all the social wrongs, but you can focus on the children and the opportunities that you have available. You have a chance to influence children's outlook now and you can sow a seed for the future. Other people will influence the children as well as you. Raising children is a long term project and you play only a temporary part.

It is crucial that children are not saddled with the responsibilities of the past and that you focus on what is happening between individual children now. For instance, a young white child cannot be held responsible for the racism in society any more than non-disabled children should carry the burden of social inequalities for disabled children and adults. You will find some books and articles which imply that offensiveness from a black child to a white is less important than the reverse, because of the reality of discrimination in society. Yet this approach is a biased and essentially adult perspective which overlooks the serious dangers of communicating to some children that their hurt matters less, for reasons over which they have no control. This mistaken approach is sometimes described as working within a hierarchy of oppression or of hurt.

Children are far more likely to appreciate social injustice towards some of their peers, when their personal concerns and hurt feelings are respected within their own social world. Children develop a strong sense of natural justice and can be very annoyed, and dismissive of adults, when they feel they have been treated unfairly.

Anti-discriminatory policy and practice

Every setting needs a clear policy on equal opportunities and guidelines for everyday practice. Any policy needs to be open to discussion and review, and an exchange of opinions within a team can raise important practical issues, as well as air misunderstandings or disagreements. Any policy can only have real meaning when it is put into practice day by day, and an equal opportunities perspective affects all the work of any centre. Equal opportunity is not a bolt-on or optional activity.

Good practice in equal opportunities is an active approach. You do not only work to remove negative views or materials but to promote a positive outlook. The idea of an **anti-bias curriculum** depends on a team's willingness to look at any imbalance in play activities or resources in their setting. The other chapters in this book look in detail at creating an even balance.

Anti-discriminatory practice is an active approach, and many different elements make up the whole framework for equal opportunities within an early years or playwork setting or a school. These elements include:

▶ A clear statement of the commitment of the setting to equal opportunities on the basis of gender, ethnic group and disability.
▶ Plans for a balanced curriculum and commitment to address any bias.
▶ A choice and range of activities for all the children, including play activities, music and dance and cultural or religious celebrations, and an awareness of the ways in which staff encourage children to use the available activities.
▶ Careful selection of all the equipment and play resources for children in the setting: books, posters, dolls, dressing-up clothes and other pretend play resources, jigsaws and craft materials.
▶ Resources for staff, including books, resource packs and training workshops.
▶ The approach to physical care of the children and an awareness of individual needs.
▶ A positive approach to children's behaviour, including harassment and bullying.
▶ Partnership with parents: explaining what you do and why, dealing with differences of opinion or deeply held beliefs.
▶ The admissions system for children, including how parents hear about possible places for their child. The system should be open, with any rules clearly explained and no restrictions that, intentionally or unintentionally, exclude children of a particular group.
▶ The selection process for staff and acceptance of volunteers in the setting.
▶ The support and supervision system.
▶ Monitoring of the range of staff, volunteers and children. If you do not reflect your local area by social or ethnic group, sex or disability, what is the reason and is this acceptable?

ACTIVITY

The written material of any setting has to be reasonably concise. Settings cannot afford to produce long documents and few parents will get round to reading pages and pages of details. So, it is almost inevitable that you will have to use brief phrases that sum up your approach. It is important that all the members of a staff team understand, and can explain what the words mean in practice in the setting. Look at the examples that follow and consider what the phrases are likely to mean in good practice:

▶ 'We celebrate diversity in the nursery.'
▶ 'Here we work to empower disabled children.'
▶ 'We respect children's home language.'
▶ 'We take a multicultural approach to caring.'
▶ 'We are committed to equality in the early years.'

Explore some phrases from the brochures of your own setting or one where you are on work placement.

Partnership with parents

PARENTS AS A RESOURCE

You will have ideas and experience within the staff team, but parents will also be a valuable source of suggestions and experience. It is important that requests for ideas or help are made in a broad way and without implying that parents are experts in a particular area because they happen to be from a minority social or ethnic group.

FOR EXAMPLE:

Patrick's parents may be knowledgeable about diabetes because of their son's condition. But they are unlikely to want to be pigeon-holed as the people who always speak up about any disability or health issue. They will want to be viewed as parents and not always as the parents of a sick child.

Be ready to ask Yan-Ling's parents for any kind of help or ideas and not only just about Chinese food or culture. Her parents may have a wide range of skills and the enthusiasm to share them with the children.

Malaika's parents may be knowledgeable about Nigeria, their family's country of origin, but they will not be experts on the entire African continent. Nigeria is also a country of great social and ethnic contrasts.

Good practice has to start with parents' first contact with your setting

Certainly it would not be good practice to be guided completely by one or two parents' views when you make decisions about play resources or activities, or even to ask, 'Now you're here, do you think we ought to get some more books or dolls?' You are not, for instance, buying jigsaws featuring disabled children just because Michael, who has cerebral palsy, has joined your setting – although to be honest, Michael's arrival may have made you acutely aware of this gap in your resources. However, the jigsaws are for everyone: for Michael and other disabled children, because they should be able to see themselves in the play materials, and for all the other children because they should have an accurately diverse view of the social world reflected in their toys.

Possible Disagreements

Your policy and practice should be clear for parents. Some conflicts or dilemmas may arise, since everyone will not agree on issues in this area. For instance, some families will hold religious or cultural beliefs that lead to firm views on how boys and girls should be treated differently. Some potential conflict may be resolved through a willingness to compromise. However, you may face some situations in which your only option is to be honest about what you do in your setting and the reasons. Parents may continue to disagree and either remove their child or regularly bring up the issue in conversation or open meetings.

Activities and resources

Resources are an important part of equal opportunities but good practice does not begin and end with the purchase of a wide range of play materials. Some resources or activities could even be counter-productive if used with limited knowledge or in a dismissive way. For instance, dolls of different ethnic backgrounds or with visible disabilities are for all the children in the group, not just for black or disabled children. It would be equally foolish to suggest that you buy blue-eyed dolls just for the blue-eyed children, or that you are postponing the decision to buy such dolls because all the children in the current group happen to have brown eyes.

A key point is balance:

▶ What images are you offering to the children?
▶ Who is present and who is missing?
▶ Can the children see themselves?
▶ Can they see other people who they might not encounter locally?
▶ Are you extending their understanding of the world beyond their neighbourhood?

There is a wide range of materials that support a positive approach to equal opportunities. But you could be forgiven for thinking there was little available, if you restrict your searches to high street toy and book stores, even in areas with a diverse local population. You will find a list of suppliers on page 193, as well as some specific ideas in each chapter.

Conversations with children

Children are curious and interested about differences and any new experiences. The best way to answer their questions is with simple and honest replies. Yet adults who deal confidently with a wide range of questions sometimes become uneasy when children's comments touch on gender, ethnic or cultural group and disability. Encouraging children to develop positive attitudes goes hand in hand with a straightforward response to their questions or reaction to their comments:

▶ Give children accurate, factual information. Sometimes, the correct answer may be along the lines of 'some people believe that . . .', rather than saying that it is, or is not, the case.
▶ Keep your replies simple, bearing in mind the child's age. If you answer questions willingly, then children will ask you again if they want more information or are puzzled. Do not try to pack long explanations into a single reply. Children lose interest if you use a simple example, for

instance, about why boys stand up to pee, to tell them all there is to know about sex differences.

▶ If you feel uncomfortable about the question, then you need to deal with these feelings, rather than pushing them onto the child with unfair comments like 'don't be nosy' or 'it's rude to stare'. Helping children to learn genuine courtesy is a different issue.

▶ Answer children's questions at the time they ask, because this is when they are interested to know. On the rare occasions when you really cannot reply, then make sure that you get back to a child with an answer.

▶ Deal simply with any offhand remarks that a child makes along with any questions. You might say, 'I don't think Zainub's head scarf is "silly". She and her Mummy wear their scarves because their family follows a tradition that women and girls cover their head.'

▶ Children may repeat offensive remarks that they have heard from other people. You will need to make a reply like, 'Yes, I know some people say that. But I think it is a rude thing to say.' Or use 'unfair', 'thoughtless' or 'wrong', depending on the context.

▶ Do not try to dodge out of giving a proper answer by evasive replies such as 'you're too young to understand', 'we're all the same inside' or 'ssh, she'll hear you'.

Children deserve honest and straightforward replies and some conventional replies are not always very helpful. For instance, children who ask, 'Why are some people black?' are sometimes told that it is because the child or adult has been in the sun or came originally from a hot country. This inaccurate reply can lead to further, reasonable questions from children about, 'Can I get very dark this summer if I stay out in the garden?' or 'Antonio is from Spain and that's a hot country, so why isn't he really dark like Rashida?' A more honest, and simpler, answer to a young child is that Rashida is dark because her parents are dark-skinned and children generally look like their parents. An older child may be ready for the explanation that everyone's skin colour depends on how much melanin you have and that you inherit this skin pigment from both your parents.

If you do not know the answer to a question, then say so, with the promise that you will find out the information. Under some circumstances, you could suggest that a child ask another child who can answer the question. Or you might perhaps check with a parent whether they could answer a query that has puzzled you. For instance, some parents of disabled children are not only familiar with fielding questions, but also have good ideas on how to explain a complex condition in simple language.

ACTIVITY

Consider the following questions and comments from children. How could you best reply to them? Discuss your ideas with colleagues or fellow students.

▶ 'Jamie says that his willy is just for having a pee. But my Mummy said that's how Daddies help to make babies. Who's right?'

▶ 'You know how you put that cream on Nneka after we go swimming? Do you do that to stop her darkness coming off?' (Nneka needs a moisturising cream otherwise her skin gets dry and cracked.)

▶ 'My uncle says people like that shouldn't go out. He says the rest of us shouldn't have to look at them.' (A comment about a group of teenagers with severe learning disabilities that children saw on a trip to the market.)

▶ 'Shall I tell you something sad? My Grandma died this weekend. Daddy says she's gone to heaven, so we shouldn't cry. Is that where Scrummy the hamster went? Is he with my Grandma?'

▶ 'Why does Marcus' Dad wear that stupid hat? My Mummy says it looks like a tea cosy.' (Marcus' family are Rastafarian and his father wears a multi-coloured tam over his dreadlocks.)

▶ 'Yvette talks funny when she's with her Daddy.' (The family is French-English bilingual.)

WHEN CHILDREN'S FEELINGS ARE HURT

Children's friends are very important to them. In nursery, playgroup or school, children are making friendships that in some cases will last for years. Adults have the responsibility to ensure that a positive environment supports children to make friends across artificial boundaries of sex, ethnic group, cultural background, language or disability.

Research into children's social and emotional development has shown that four- and five-year-olds can show empathy towards their peers and altruistic behaviour (a selfless willingness to help and support others). This development does not follow automatically with the passing of the months and years. Children learn from how adults behave and from the encouragement that they offer.

Sometimes what children say will directly affect another child. It is unfair to the hurt child if adults ignore the incident, and an opportunity is lost to help the other child to grasp that what he or she said was hurtful and unnecessary.

Children whose feelings have been hurt do not usually want the other child to be told off, especially if the result is that they are blamed later for getting their peer into trouble. So, adults are looking for a subtle balance between acknowledging what has happened and that some remarks are unacceptable, but not making such a fuss from the child's point of view that any lessons are lost. The following ideas are guidelines for your positive reaction but are not rules to be followed in every case, and certainly not in a way that would make your reaction very lengthy.

A child who has been on the receiving end of a hurtful or offensive remark deserves and needs:

▶ Comfort, through your words or friendly touch, if they wish. A child who has been very hurt by another's words, or persistent verbal bullying, may be close to tears and welcome a cuddle.
▶ An acknowledgement that the remark was 'unfair', 'untrue', 'cruel' or another appropriate word.
▶ A clear message from you that you like them and feel positive about any source of identity that has been under verbal attack. Be guided by the child's own feelings and what you have learned about them. For instance, some disabled children or those with continuing health problems do not feel comforted by words that they are 'a special child'. Their condition does not feel special to them in any positive way and they may want empathy about their frustrations.
▶ Reassurance that no child has to tolerate verbal bullying or name calling in order to be accepted by the group. Children should not have to take a so-called joke against themselves. Certainly the key point about a joke, or a bit of fun, is that everyone enjoys it, not that some children find it amusing and others are distressed.

Children who have given hurt or offence need to understand that:

▶ The remark was unacceptable, with an explanation if they seem puzzled about the fuss. You can say honestly that, 'That's not a word I like to hear in this nursery' or, 'I don't want you to call Kenny a spas.' This direct approach is more likely to work well than trying to make the child feel guilty with, 'Don't you think that was a hurtful thing to say!'
▶ You can disapprove of what a child might have said but you still like them. So, you say, ' I think that was a rude name to call Sara' rather than, 'You are such a rude child!' Keep the behaviour separate from the child as a person – in your mind and through what you say.
▶ Listen to the child who is being offensive. Perhaps you can sort out the

conflict that led to the insults. You may sometimes be able to sympathise with a child's frustrations, whilst saying, 'It's still not okay for you to call Nathan "coconut".'

► Encourage the children to consider the feelings of their peers. Some children may be more ready to empathise than others, especially if they too have been on the receiving end of insults.

► Sometimes, children's view of a situation is inaccurate. Perhaps a child says that Harry has one arm shorter than the other because 'he's such a bad boy'. You will need to say, 'Harry was born with his shorter arm. It's nothing to do with being good or bad.'

► A child's remark can sometimes be corrected courteously, so that they can learn something. Perhaps children are making fun of two girls whom they do not understand. You might explain, 'Teja and Leela aren't speaking rubbish. They can speak Hindi as well as English. They have two languages.'

There may be opportunities to support positive behaviour between children through other parts of your early years curriculum. Books and story telling, puppet play or simple drama and role play all offer possibilities for exploring feelings and how children should treat one another in general. It will be important that no child feels that a story or puppet play is directly linked with a recent altercation between individual children, and certainly not that she or he is being criticised yet again for an incident that was supposed to be finished.

As children get older, some of them may ask you searching questions about the inequalities within society or why some people are so hurtful to other adults or children for no good reason. Make your answers straightforward and avoid overwhelming children with too much social or historical information in one conversation. They will come back to you when they want to know more. Unfortunately, you will have to be honest and admit that life is sometimes cruelly unfair.

FOR EXAMPLE:

My daughter, Tanith, was eight years old when she asked me some very pointed questions about racism. Her friend Leela had told her how a man from the upper floor of a nearby block of flats shouted racist abuse at her on many afternoons as she walked home below the block. Tanith was distressed on Leela's behalf and could not grasp why anyone, especially an adult, would be so horrible to a child who had done nothing wrong. I explained some of the background to racism in simple terms, but Tanith still returned to the individual basis of the almost daily incident: why was a complete stranger shouting at Leela just because she was Asian?

Young children's concern about why individuals are horrible to other individuals is an important focus that adults should not lose. Positive attitudes for children can be grounded in their feelings for their friends and their understanding of how they might feel, or have felt, in similar circumstances.

The law and equal opportunities

How laws work

Laws create a framework for people's behaviour by defining some boundaries around what must, or must not, be done. Legislation does not automatically change behaviour or attitudes, but it does make a public statement about what is acceptable or unacceptable within a society.

Views of good practice have developed since the 1950s and 1960s – and will continue to develop

The laws described in this section are **primary legislation** and the requirements built into the laws must be obeyed. However, legal language is not expressed in a way that allows straightforward application to daily life. Sometimes the relevant government department issues further information through books of **guidance** or **codes of practice**. These documents do not have the same force as primary legislation, but it is expected that local authorities or relevant organisations will follow the details of guidance or a code. In the years after a new law has been passed, there may be court cases that test parts of that law that are open to more than one interpretation. Legal decisions following a disagreement provide a resource of **case law**, that sets definite **precedents** for when a similar disagreement arises in the future.

Good Practice and the Law

Good practice in equal opportunities is considerably broader than the requirements of any of the laws described here. Even all the fine detail of laws will not cover everything in your setting. Good practice in any area of work with children has to pay attention to legal requirements, but the details of how you work are also shaped by an understanding of children, how they develop and learn. Knowledge about child development continues to expand and practical applications of research can shape a review of good practice. Good practice is also influenced and changed over time by the impact of experience and sharing ideas within the early years, play work and educational professions.

The Sex Discrimination Acts 1975 and 1986

The legislation contained within these Acts was in response to widespread discrimination against women, in terms of employment and pay, use of services or in reference to a woman's marital status. The Equal Opportunities Commission (address on page 72) monitors the Sex Discrimination Acts.

The Acts make it illegal to discriminate against people on the grounds of their sex. Although the law was introduced in response to discrimination against women, the requirements apply equally to males and females. So, no early years setting can decide to turn away any male applicants for posts, any more than a company can refuse to employ women. Treating someone less favourably just because of their sex would be a form of **direct discrimination** and therefore illegal.

Sometimes discriminatory behaviour is less obvious. **Indirect discrimination** is also illegal and occurs when, for instance, an employer applies a condition to a job or rules for promotion that mean that one sex is considerably less likely to be able to meet the condition. Exceptions can be only be made if the sex of a worker can be justified as a genuine occupational qualification. Special encouragement or training can be offered to people of a sex under-represented in an area of work, but employers cannot discriminate positively at the point of offering a job, for example by having a quota.

The Race Relations Act 1976

The Act was a response to substantial discrimination on racial grounds within British society and the aim of the law was to define discrimination and make such behaviour illegal. The Commission for Racial Equality (address on page 122) continues to monitor the application of the Race Relations Act.

The Act made it unlawful to discriminate on racial grounds, which cover skin colour, race, nationality including citizenship, ethnic or national origins. Religious affiliation is not included in the definition. Case law has further established that some groups are, or are not, defined as a distinct racial group. For instance, cases brought to court have established that Sikhs and travellers are distinct ethnic groups and so are covered by the Act.

Discriminatory behaviour was defined in four broad ways. The following examples have been made relevant to early years, but the legislation is applicable to the whole society.

▶ *Direct discrimination* – for instance, refusing to admit a child to a nursery because he was Chinese or to employ a new member of staff because she was Egyptian. The Act applies to everyone, so an all-Asian staff group could not just decide that they did not want any non-Asian colleagues.
▶ *Indirect discrimination* – applying any condition that in practice favours one group over another. Groups that judge they need a worker of a particular ethnic group have to justify the need on non-racial grounds, for instance, a bilingual worker to support bilingual children.
▶ *Segregation* – for instance, a classroom organised so that children from traveller families had to sit on a different table to other children (and there was no genuine care or educational reason for this pattern).
▶ *Victimisation* – if children were excluded from pre-school, or treated badly by staff, as a result of complaints by their parents about earlier discrimination.

The Race Relations Act is not concerned with people's motives or intentions; the focus is entirely on what happens as a result of behaviour or organisational rules put into practice. Like any law, the Act does not enable anyone to insist that a person or group has acted illegally without offering definite proof. Any possible prosecutions only go forward after careful consideration of evidence.

For further information on the Race Relations Act:
Lane, Jane (1996) *From Cradle to School: a practical guide to racial equality in early childhood education and care* (Commission for Racial Equality)

The Children Act 1989

The Act arose from considerable concern that existing legislation was confusing and did not create an appropriate balance between protection of children and parents' rights. The primary aims of the Act were to protect children, prevent family breakdown and to ensure minimum standards in services for children and their families.

So, the Children Act is not primarily a piece of equal opportunities legislation but some parts, supported by government guidance (see below), have established a positive framework for good practice. The aim was to promote good practice as well as to establish that any service must meet minimum standards below which it should not be allowed to fall. The relevant aspects to standards relating to equal opportunities are:

► Minimum standards require that services for children and their families take positive account of individual children's **'religious persuasion, racial origin and cultural and linguistic background'** (this is the key phrase used in the Act). Evidence of refusal to take account of these issues is one reason given within the Act, for refusing or cancelling the registration of a day care provider.

► The requirements of the Act focus on the individuality of the actual children attending relevant services. However, the Department of Health's guidance makes the more general point about all children learning positive attitudes, regardless of the exact composition of their group.

► The Children Act itself does not mention children's sex, although the guidance adds this issue as part of children's individuality.

► Local authorities were required to organise or provide services for children defined as being 'in need'. Disabled children were specifically included in that definition.

For further information on the Children Act:

Department of Health (1991) *The Children Act 1989 Guidance and Regulations, Volume 2, Family Support, Day Care and Educational Provision for Young Children* (HMSO)

Elfer, Peter (1991) *The Children Act and Day Care* (National Children's Bureau, Highlight no. 100)

Elfer, Peter (1995) *With Equal Concern* (National Children's Bureau)

Smith, Peter (1989) *Overview of the Children Act 1989* (National Children's Bureau, Highlight no. 91)

Legislation and disability

There have been a series of Education Acts that affect disabled children and their families. Brief highlights are given here of the main changes brought about by the laws. The Children Act 1989 was also relevant to disabled children – see the previous section.

The Education Act 1981

This Act introduced the concept of **special educational needs** that focused on the learning needs of children (as opposed to a label of handicapped). Local authorities were obligated to meet children's learning needs through special educational provision and a process leading to a **statement** of special educational needs was established. The Act also recognised the central role of parents in choices offered and decisions made about their children.

The Education Reform Act 1988

The 1988 Act established a national curriculum for all children, including those with special educational needs. The Act confirmed the move towards inclusion of disabled children in mainstream schooling, with any variations made with regard to the individual needs of a child.

The Education Act 1993

This built on the 1981 Act. The details of the 1993 Act form the current legislation that applies to disabled children and services for them. The Code of Practice issued in 1994 offers guidance on the standards that are required for local education authorities to implement the provisions of the 1993 Act. The Code requires, for instance, that:

▶ professionals work in partnership with parents
▶ listen to the children's preferences
▶ have a special educational needs policy

▶ identify and assess children
▶ maintain a register of children with special educational needs.

THE EDUCATION ACT 1996

This changed a few titles for sections of the Act, but the legal requirements remain essentially the same.

For further information about the law and disabled children:

Dare, Angela and Donovan, Margaret (1997) *Good Practice in Caring for Young Children with Special Needs* (Stanley Thornes)

Department of Health (1991) *The Children Act 1989 Guidance and Regulations, Volume 6, Children with Disabilities* (HMSO)

Russell, Philippa (1992) *The Children Act 1989 and disability* (National Children's Bureau, Highlight no. 109)

Russell, Philippa (1995) *The code of practice: Education Act 1993* (National Children's Bureau, Highlight no. 132)

Stobbs, Philippa (1993) *The Education Act 1993 and special educational needs* (National Children's Bureau, Highlight no. 123)

2

Good practice with girls and boys

Gender and society

All cultures take a stance on how to raise girls and boys to ensure that they grow into the women and men that the society or cultural group wants and expects. British society is no exception to this general rule and, until recent decades, the pattern was clearly one in which men and boys were more highly valued than women and girls. Most of this chapter will be about current practice, but equal opportunities in relation to gender does not make real sense without some history.

Use of words

A number of words and phrases are often used in discussion of equal opportunities and gender.

▶ **Sex** and **sex differences** are used to refer to the biological difference between boys and girls, and men and women. Good practice in equal opportunities is not to deny that such a difference exists but to question some of the assumptions and expectations that follow.

▶ **Gender** is used to describe the social identity of being male or female. For instance, **gender appropriate** activities are judged to be right for one sex but not another, because of social beliefs about males and females.

▶ **Stereotypes** are firm beliefs about the characteristics of a given group and its individual members. A sex role or gender stereotype includes views about what women and men, boys and girls, are like in behaviour, talents or weaknesses.

▶ **Sexism** is an outlook of prejudiced attitudes and discriminatory behaviour towards individuals on the basis of their sex, usually arising from the beliefs in a stereotype. An **anti-sexist** approach aims to counteract the impact of sexism and encourage fairer attitudes and behaviour. Much discussion about sexism has focused on unfair treatment of women and girls. However, a rounded anti-sexist approach must be even-handed with attention to boys as well as girls.

The historical background

During the first half of the twentieth century, laws and entrenched social attitudes encouraged a view that females were less able, less responsible and less important in society than men. The decades from the end of the nineteenth century and into the first part of the twentieth saw some improvement, from a situation in which women had scarcely higher legal status than children, to one in which some basic rights, including being able to vote, were granted to them. However, many legal and social inequalities continued into the second half of the century – well within the memory of many people with whom you can talk now.

HOME AND WORK

Females were expected to care for their families and raise children. Although this role was supposedly respected, many other messages to women and girls told them loudly that the male role was considerably more valuable. Women taking family responsibility were routinely dismissed as 'just a housewife'. Women were judged to be less intelligent and more emotional (meant as a criticism) than men. Into the 1970s some official paperwork was still sent out with the instruction that, 'If you are a married woman, your husband should complete this form as if it were addressed to him.' It seems very normal now to have female news readers, but I recall firm statements made during the 1960s that 'nobody would ever take the news seriously read by a woman'.

Girls were expected to do less well in their education and many people argued against further education for girls on the grounds that they would only get married. During the 1950s and into the 1960s, it was accepted that women had to resign from professional jobs when they got married. The view that married women should not work overlooked the long tradition of working women in many factories and mills. It was considered reasonable that females should be paid less than males although they were doing an identical job. The assumption was that men had, or would soon have, a family to support and that women just worked for extras (the phrase used was 'pin money'). This situation was changed in the 1970s and 1980s by equal pay and sexual discrimination legislation. Some of the social attitudes still persist.

SOCIAL RESEARCH AND THEORY

During the twentieth century, broad social attitudes about men and women were reflected in the social sciences, despite their claim to be objective. Most of the well-known names from early psychology and sociology were men and few people questioned their built-in assumptions that the male perspective was the rational and right outlook.

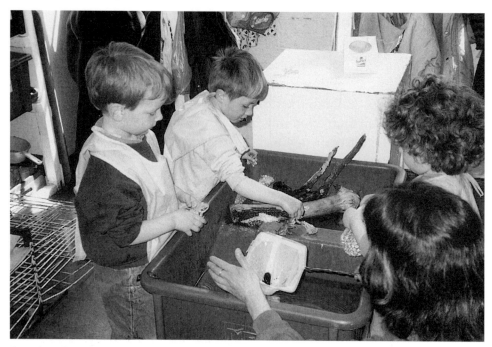

Sometimes boys and girls will play together

Theories about personality development, moral reasoning and behaviour patterns such as aggression, often took observations of men or boys as the norm. When a theory did not easily apply to female development or behaviour, the reaction was rarely to re-think the theory. The explanation was far more often that the female pattern was a deviation from 'normal' development or a sign of problems. Books with titles like *Human Aggression* would cover almost exclusively male behaviour. During the 1970s, there was a strong reaction against this bias within social sciences. Many female psychologists and sociologists worked to make society value the different female patterns and to build theory and research that was a genuine reflection of both sexes.

EQUAL OPPORTUNITIES IN EARLY YEARS

Given the historical background, it is not surprising that the first concern of the feminist movement in the 1960s and 1970s was to gain equality for women on many issues. Similarly, the first focus in applying ideas to childhood addressed how girls were being given messages that would restrict their options and development. Those involved in any movement about good practice must be ready to reflect and that is what has happened with equal opportunities in relation to gender. More recently, there has been an increasing awareness of the messages being given to boys and the possible negative effects on their development.

POSSIBLE DILEMMAS

There are parallels between equal opportunities in relation to gender and equal opportunities to do with ethnic group and cultural tradition (see Chapter 3). But the two areas of good practice are not the same and some dilemmas can arise. In fact, some aspects of good practice in gender equal opportunities challenge many cultural traditions, including British traditions. In some settings it will be impossible to develop good practice in your treatment of girls and boys **and** to follow every parent's preferences. Some cultures, and social groups within a culture, express deeply held beliefs that boys and girls should be treated differently and will be resistant to your approach. A team can address this potential conflict between equal opportunities and partnership with parents in several ways:

▶ Be clear and honest in your policy statements about how you aim to treat boys and girls and why equal opportunity is a positive issue in your setting.
▶ Be ready to talk with parents about what you do and why, and also what you do not do. For instance, you are not saying that girls and boys are all the same, nor are you banning traditional activities.
▶ Some parents will agree with your approach or see the value when you explain. Others, from a variety of cultural backgrounds, may continue to disagree. You will show respect for parents' views by listening and demonstrating that you wish to understand their point of view. However, what some parents want may be against centre policy and you have to be honest about that reality. It will be the parents' choice whether their child continues to attend your setting.

It is useful to remember that parents will not agree with all your methods or principles, not just on equal opportunities. Sometimes you will hear about the disagreement, but sometimes you will never realise, because the parents decide that they are mainly satisfied with the setting and are willing to compromise on a given issue. An important element in a genuine partnership with parents will be how you deal, courteously and honestly, with situations in which you do not agree on the approach or priorities.

Focus on the children

There are three related questions about the development of boys and girls and these issues are often muddled in conversation or argument on the topic:

1 Are boys and girls different from each other? If so, then in what way(s)?

2 If boys and girls are consistently different, is this explained by inborn differences, from what they learn during childhood, or from some combination of the two possibilities?
3 Should girls and boys be different from each other in behaviour, outlook or aspirations? Is it part of adults' responsibility to encourage girls and boys to be different?

The first question addresses the common belief that the two sexes are different enough to justify comments such as 'girls always talk earlier' and 'boys are more adventurous'. The second question homes in on the possible explanations of any differences. The final question relates to values: 'should boys and girls be different?' rather than, 'are they different?' Some cultural traditions promote a very clear division between male and female roles in life and encourage development of the differences in early childhood. In some cultures, or groups within a culture, expectations for girls and boys may have much in common. But there may still be subtle differences in how the sexes are treated and assumptions about appropriate behaviour in adult life. Beliefs that girls and boys should behave differently often shape adults' interpretations of what they observe children saying or doing.

Are boys and girls different from each other?

Of course, in one important way girls and boys are very different from each other. Girls grow up into young women and boys grow into young men. This transformation happens at puberty. Part of children's growing sense of personal identity must include a positive outlook on the adults they will eventually become. But it is another issue when people consider that many other differences, including personality and behaviour, follow the sex difference in a predictable way.

DIFFERENT OR BETTER?

It has been difficult to discuss sex differences in a calm way, because for so long any apparent differences between females and males were interpreted in a biased way, usually as evidence that females were in some way inferior.

For many years, girls' greater achievements in the early years of school were explained away by the view that boys were later developers. There are even indications that, during the 1950s and 1960s when all children sat the 11+ examination, the pass level was made tougher for girls in some authorities, because otherwise there would have been significantly more girls in the local grammar schools than boys. Yet girls' under achievement in maths and science at secondary level was taken as proof that females were poor at subjects requiring objectivity or logic. Many of the current generation of adults grew up hearing that women should not be in positions of responsibility because they were too emotional. Yet aggressive behaviour in boys or men was not thought of as a dubious emotional reaction. The behaviour was more likely to be interpreted as a sign of strength, or of leadership potential.

There are some signs that attitudes are changing. People are gradually accepting that all parts of society, not least children, need a blend of perspectives and abilities, some of which may be more on the masculine side and some on the feminine. 'Different' does not necessarily mean better or worse, superior or inferior.

Are There Any Consistent Differences Between Girls and Boys?

Careful research into children's development and behaviour has established no absolute differences between boys and girls in their development or behaviour. There is no basis for saying that *all* boys are better at particular skills or that *all* girls behave in a particular way. The sexes' different patterns at puberty are the only exception and there is still great variety between individual males and females at this stage of development. So, the question has to be whether on balance, boys generally show more or less of a characteristic or a tendency than girls.

If a consistent difference is found when studying groups of children, the sex difference is usually small. For instance, some but not all studies of aggression in children have shown a greater tendency of boys towards aggressiveness, but the average difference between the sexes is still small. There is **no** basis for saying that most boys are more aggressive than most girls. You can **only** say that in a large group of children, the most aggressive individuals are more likely to be boys than girls.

Observation and assessment of children have shown a great deal of variety between individuals of the same sex and that, in many ways, girls and boys are more similar than unlike. Both sexes are represented across the spectrum of development, behaviour, abilities and difficulties.

There are, for example, three to four times as many boys with dyslexia as girls. So, if you are working in the early years of school, you could expect to encounter more boys with this learning disability than girls. But it would be poor practice to overlook this possibility for girls, because some females are dyslexic. Furthermore, you cannot assume that most boys will have difficulties, because some will be enthusiastic and skilled readers.

Study of language development has suggested that, on average, girls tend to talk more and in slightly longer sentences than boys in early childhood. This average difference lasts into middle childhood when, girls, as a group, do slightly better than boys on verbal reasoning and brain teasers based on words. On the other hand, boys, as a group, show a slightly stronger flair for problems that require numerical reasoning. I keep using the phrases 'as a group' and 'on average' because these slightly different patterns do not allow anyone to predict that individual children will be better at the skills. Some girls will be stronger on numerical reasoning than some boys, in the same way that some boys will be more articulate in their language than some of their female peers.

How do differences arise?

It is very difficult to find out which differences between male and female children are the result of biology (nature) and which are the result of the different ways in which girls and boys are treated from their earliest days (nurture). It seems likely that some combination of the two factors is at work and not necessarily the same mix for all possible characteristics. Adults who believe that girls and boys should be different (the third question on page 36) will encourage children towards some kinds of behaviour, and discourage them from others, on the basis of a child's sex.

Research into aggressive patterns of behaviour suggests an interplay between nature and nurture. Many studies have shown that, from a young age, boys tend to hit and insult each other more than girls. Boys also tend to react more swiftly and strongly if they are hit or insulted. Boys are more likely than girls to engage in general rough and tumble, and play fighting. The observation that the physically more aggressive pattern emerges so young in boys, raises the possibility of some biological basis to their behaviour. However, observation of adults with children has shown that they are very likely to behave differently towards very young children, even babies, depending on the child's sex. Boys are more likely to be encouraged towards active physical behaviour (which is not necessarily aggressive) and adults seem to tolerate more dominant or aggressive behaviour in boys before it is regarded as a problem.

Adult assumptions about how children should behave shape their expectations of what children will do and their interpretations of children's behaviour. The first question asked by many adults when faced with a young baby is the sex and then baby's behaviour is often interpreted in line with whether they are a boy or girl. Anecdotal evidence suggests that adults think crying girl babies need comfort and cuddling, whereas crying boy babies need some physical action and distraction.

FOR EXAMPLE:

When our son, Drew, was a few months old we visited friends who had older children – Maggie who was six years old and Tim who was eight years. Maggie moved immediately towards Drew, touched him gently and asked to hold him. Tim looked on with interest but from a slight distance. As Maggie cuddled Drew, her father said confidently that this only went to show that girls were more interested in babies – it came naturally. At that point, the children's mother spoke up and said that perhaps Tim was interested as well. Tim nodded firmly in agreement and asked if he could also have a turn to hold Drew. Soon Tim took his sister's place and showed just as much interest and care in cuddling and talking with our very young baby. It was hard not to conclude that Tim was holding back because of his father's remarks (not the first time we had heard this type of comment) and, without his mother's intervention, Tim's reticence would have proved his father's claim.

▶ Bear in mind that individual boys and girls may well vary in their interest and inclinations, but their options will be restricted if adults assume that children will, or will not, want to explore a particular opportunity.
▶ Watch out for examples of how adult beliefs and expectations could encourage or discourage children in different situations.

ACTIVITY

Whatever research suggests, there is no doubt that many people believe that girls and boys are reliably different. Over a period of two to three weeks, listen into conversations in your working and personal life and gather examples of firm views on such differences. You might hear that 'girl babies are so much easier' or 'he's into everything – a real boy'.

Look over the examples you have gathered and, if possible, compare with colleagues or fellow students who have completed the same activity.

▶ What images are emerging of girls and boys?

▶ How did any of the speakers deal with disagreement? For instance, somebody might have said, 'Well I had a much harder time when my daughter was a baby. My son was the easy one.'
▶ In what ways do you think any of the speakers' actions might enforce or prove their beliefs?

Awareness of your own behaviour

Resources and activities are an important part of equal opportunities in practice but your own language and behaviour are just as important.

Your own learning

Young children are not the only people to have been influenced by social expectations of the two sexes. You, your colleagues, parents and all other adults have been influenced during childhood. There is no need to feel apologetic, or that you are to blame for learned assumptions and expectations. You are not responsible for the actions of adults in your childhood. On the other hand, you are responsible now for thinking about your views, being willing to question some of them and to adjust how you behave towards young children.

Children look towards adults for guidance on what is a normal or generally acceptable way to behave. Children need input from adults of both sexes and they look towards the adults of their sex for an idea of what it is to be a grown-up. What you say matters, but your actions speak as loudly as your words. Fine sentiments of 'girls can do anything that boys can' will be undermined if children see females acting as if they are hopeless and cannot learn when faced with a 'traditionally' male task.

> FOR EXAMPLE:
>
> Children mainly learn from what they experience directly, so they will not learn gender stereotypes if they observe a different pattern.
>
> In a family I know, the mother works as an electrical engineer and the father in management. The children are used to their mother tackling anything electrical in the house and this is normal life as far as they are concerned. On one occasion their father was in charge of the children and a kitchen appliance needed a new plug. As soon as the children saw

their father with a screwdriver, they became concerned: did Daddy know what he was doing? Mummy did plugs and everything like that, shouldn't he wait until she got home? Their father persevered and changed the plug but was watched by two anxious children who could not wait to tell their mother and be reassured that everything was alright.

▶ Until they have a broader experience, children tend to assume that everyone's family life runs in a similar way to their own. Do you have examples of your own, where children's conversation shows how they are generalising from their own life?

▶ It is possible for children to experience a family life in which gender stereotypes are not strictly followed and yet *still* learn a traditional view about what mothers and fathers do and do not do. Perhaps they have a working mother but still say 'mummies stay at home'. How do you think this happens?

Equal opportunities in practice

Any setting concerned about equal opportunities and gender should consider the following:

▶ How are boys and girls treated during the session or day? Are there patterns (intended or not) that are different, depending on whether a child is a girl or a boy?

▶ How do workers behave? What do they say about children or about their own, adult abilities? What role model do the children gain from the adults?

▶ What activities are available and how are children encouraged, or discouraged, to use them?

▶ What resources are available for children and what kind of world do they show?

Children's individuality

Obviously, children's sex is part of their identity. Good practice would not be to treat all children the same, nor to pretend that the sex difference does not exist. The aim of equal opportunities in practice is to open doors for children, not to close them, to encourage children to extend their talents and knowledge without feeling restricted by beliefs about 'that's for girls' or 'boys don't do that'.

A POSITIVE SENSE OF IDENTITY

Your aim is for both sexes to feel positive about their own identity. Girls' views of their skills and strengths need to be far removed from any sense of 'being just a girl'. Everyone will be good at some skills and not so good at others. Adult support is important to make sure that children do not believe they are good at a skill 'because I'm a girl' or that there is no point in trying 'because only boys are good at that'. Children and adults must appreciate individual strengths and weaknesses.

Girls need confidence and self-esteem, but boys too need a positive sense of themselves and their interests. In a society that still tends to value male pre-occupations and values over female, it is important that boys develop a sense of self-worth that is personal, not one dependent on a mistaken belief in male superiority. Inevitably, because of social pressures and inborn differences, boys and girls will show some different patterns of play activity and everyday skills such as problem solving. It is important that early years care and education workers (most of whom are, after all, female) ensure that equal opportunities remain equal and boys' interests are shown to be valued.

Adults have a large responsibility for what they say and do because these actions give powerful messages to children. Children listen, even when you are not talking directly to them, and they watch what you do. From their observations, children build up attitudes about how the different sexes behave, or are expected to behave. Children can develop firm views of what boys and girls can do or cannot do, should do and should not do, what is possible and what is hard or impossible. Babies are not born with a set of attitudes about gender; these views are learned. Of course, children do not accept all the messages from their environment, and sometimes they have to make choices because they are given inconsistent messages from different adults or from friends.

Your use of language

Your words reflect your attitudes about gender and how you feel it is appropriate to react to boys and girls. Within any team it is worth listening out for what you all say. This section includes some examples for you to consider:

▶ Do your words tend to give particular messages to the children? For example, 'I want some helpful girls to lay the table with me' or, 'I'm looking for two strong boys to shift these boxes.' Perhaps you could express a request in a more open way, for instance, 'I would like some help with laying the table' or, 'These boxes are heavy, I would appreciate two or three children to help me move them.' Most children like to help and both sexes will benefit from learning about domestic routines or the care needed when moving heavier objects.

▶ Do you tend to compliment girls more on their appearance (hair style or clothes) and boys more on skills or strength? What words do you use with boys and girls? Are they different and, if so, why?

TO THINK ABOUT

Some children like adults to notice when they have a new hair cut or they may be very pleased with their new coat. But you probably need to consider compliments about appearance with some care, since some children may not have many new clothes. Compliments can be more general, and not gender specific, if you make comments like, 'That jumper looks good on you', 'What a lovely colour' or, 'That coat looks really cosy for this cold weather.'

▶ Are you tempted to tell boys to be 'careful' under different circumstances from similar warnings to girls? Perhaps you are inclined to tell girls to watch out on the climbing frame or even to suggest 'that's too high' at an earlier stage than you would for a boy. On the other hand, are the boys more likely to be watched and told 'now be very careful' if they are doing something domestic or handling a breakable item? Do your words show that you tend to make a different assessment about risk, depending on the sex of a child?

▶ Do you catch yourself expressing surprise about what individual children have done, because of their sex? Perhaps you are more fulsome in your praise when a girl has built something mechanical or when a boy has made a pretend meal out of play dough. All children need encouragement and individual children deserve that extra boost when they have managed something that did not come easily. But children will often sense the hidden message that is more about gender stereotypes than individual achievement.

▶ Do your words reflect an expectation that boys and girls will most likely have a different pattern of interests and concerns? For instance, do you expect that the boys are more likely to be interested in the library book about mechanical diggers and the girls in the book about baby animals? Of course, you may well observe some differences in interests, but children can have learned that diggers are more for boys and cute animals for girls. However, your words could reinforce this idea and make it harder for the children to develop new interests.

▶ Do you make assumptions about children's likely difficulties or talents? For instance, do you express surprise that a boy is not keen to get his hands dirty, when a girl's reluctance might be understood? Do you find yourself making suggestions to help a girl to put pieces together in a construction, when you would probably let a boy make his own choices? Or do you expect to tell a boy how to lay the table in the home corner or how to help you to prepare for tea, whereas you would probably assume a girl would know what to do?

▶ Are you more likely to ask a girl to watch over a newly arrived child, a younger one or a disabled child? If you ask a boy to help in this way, are you tempted to give more guidance than you would with a girl?

▶ Do your words imply that it is normal for boys to be noisy by saying, 'If you want to play a noisy game, go outside.' But if it is a group of girls you suggest, 'Can you play the game more quietly?'

▶ Do you place a different interpretation on an incident, depending on whether a child is a boy or a girl? What happens if a child is crying? Do you, or your colleagues, make different comments if the child is a boy, perhaps trying to jolly him out of it? What happens when children come to blows? Are adults' reactions different if the fighters are all boys, or all girls? If the children are in a mixed group, are there assumptions about who started the fisticuffs?

▶ Are boys allowed to interrupt conversations or to shout out in story time, but girls are more likely to be asked to wait or to talk in a normal voice? (Some research suggests that this happens in school.) Are boys who interrupt most likely to be viewed as confident or keen, whereas girls may be described as impatient or pushy?

▶ You should be wary of describing the same, or very similar, behaviour in different ways just because the child is a girl or a boy. A child who is a confident organiser and leader in a group is not bossy just because she is female. A child who is sensitive to events and easily moved to tears is not immature because he is a boy. If in doubt, think about whether you would use this description about a child of the opposite sex and same age. If not, do you have any sound reason for saying it about this child?

A POSITIVE APPROACH IN A TEAM

The aim is to be thoughtful about what you say, to talk about the meaning of words and the ideas they express. Everyone should take an approach that will open up children's opportunities, rather than close them down. A team that has become very aware of these issues may wish to alert volunteers or parent helpers to the impact of what they say to boys and girls. (See also the general suggestions about language on page 42.)

Discussion between colleagues in one-to-one conversations, or in whole staff groups, needs to give people room to think. Workers should not be pushed into a position where they are too busy defending themselves to consider the real issues. Positive approaches could include the following:

▶ 'What makes you say that?' rather than, 'You mustn't say that!'
▶ 'Please explain to me why you think we should stop the boys' super heroes game.'
▶ 'These comments just pop out, don't they? I couldn't believe what I nearly said to Kimberly the other day. Perhaps we need to think about what we're bringing to our time with the children.'
▶ 'I agree with what you say about Angela's behaviour. But I'm not sure that we can explain what she does just by saying that she's a girl. What about how her mother talks with her? We were discussing that the other day . . .'
▶ 'Yes I know that Barry and Daniel are hogging the bikes. But are we being fair to say that there's a problem because boys won't share? What about Alric or Terry? They seem to be willing to take their turns.'

ACTIVITY

When adults describe children, they do not use an identical vocabulary for girls and boys. Some words carry a different meaning (positive or negative), depending on the sex of the child to whom they are applied. Consider the following list of words, perhaps discuss them with a colleague or fellow student.

If you think a word is mainly used to describe boys then write it under a list you head with B. If you think it is mostly applied to girls, then list under G. Any words that you think are used fairly evenly between the two sexes, list under E.

Pretty	Tough	Curious
Cooperative	Sensitive	Rough
Strong	Shy	Affectionate
Clever	Talkative	Sensible
Sturdy	Nice	Thoughtful
Dainty	Adventurous	Patient
Active	Creative	Caring
Handsome	Alert	Loud
Cautious	Dependable	Careless
Confident	Outgoing	Sweet
Helpful	Brave	Quick

▶ Discuss the three lists you have made and consider how your use of words may give clear messages to children which might also be reflected in other aspects of your behaviour.

▶ Try applying a word from your B list to girls. How does it sound and feel to you? Now try the opposite, with a word from your G list applied to boys.

▶ Consider three practical steps you could take to improve your use of words with girls and boys.

Children's play and behaviour

What they say

Children will listen to what you say and learn from you but, of course, they will also bring views into your setting from their own family life and what they see on television. Sometimes their views, expressed in words and actions, will support the approach to equal opportunities taken in your setting. However, some of the children's views will be at odds with the atmosphere you are working to create:

▶ Children may be ready to criticise the opposite sex as 'no good' or 'useless'. They may express views that are rejecting of the opposite sex and restrict what they can or should be doing. Children may also use disdainful or offensive terms about other children on the basis of their sex: cissy or fairy, slag or bitch. Neither sex should be allowed to bad mouth the other and no worker should let themselves believe that it matters less if the girls are being offensive to the boys than the other way around.

▶ Children may bring in views that they apply to themselves. For instance, Daniel says, 'I shouldn't play with the dolls, my Dad says that's for cissies' or Angela says, 'I can't go up there. My Mum says girls are no good at climbing. I'll fall and hurt myself.'

▶ Children may express views that are based on limited information and their own experience. They may be confident that 'all boys' or 'all Mummies' do something and have no idea of the variety in the groups.

It is important that you treat children's views with respect and do not dismiss what they say in a way that could make the children unwilling to express opinions to you in the future. A courteous approach can be blended with a positive attempt to help children to think further.

Listen to what children have to say, do not reject their views out of hand, or bluntly tell them they are wrong or rude. You would not appreciate this approach and it is inappropriate for children. Nor it is helpful to label children's remarks as 'sexist'. Labelling and dismissing what children say does not help them to learn. It may also encourage them to use the term against each other, just because opposing sides of an argument are held by children of the opposite sex. Groups of older children, because they have not really been helped to discuss and resolve disagreements, may take the quick and easy route of calling each other 'sexist' or 'racist'. You can encourage a more positive approach from the early years.

Your actions in dealing with offensive or dismissive remarks should be similar whether the offensiveness is based on a child's sex, ethnic group, disability or any feature of a child's personal identity or experience. There are times for ignoring minor misbehaviour, but it is unwise to let offensiveness pass without comment. When a child is sure that you heard, your silence will be taken as acceptance, or even approval, of what was said. Mild, non-specific reprimands are not usually that helpful, because they do not give children much of an explanation. Vague comments such as 'that's not a nice thing to say' or 'that's not fair' do not offer a child much information. A more specific challenge that still leaves a child some room to reply can be more effective. For example:

► You can question the absolute truth of what a child is saying, without saying bluntly, 'you're wrong'.
► You should also avoid putting children in an uncomfortable position by claiming that someone who matters to them is wrong. For instance, your reply to Angela (whose mother thinks girls cannot climb) might be, 'Well, I've come across a lot of girls who are really good climbers. Why don't you try climbing just up to there. I'll be standing right here.' Your reply to Daniel (whose dad thinks boys should not like dolls) could be, 'I know some people feel the same way as your Dad, but I don't agree. I think you can enjoy playing with dolls and still be a proper boy.'
► You may say firmly that you do not want to hear certain words or phrases. You can explain by saying, 'I think that is a rude word to use about another person and I don't want to hear you use it any more.' You might need to add that you realise that the word was used in a television programme or film but, 'I still don't want to hear you say it in the nursery, please.' This approach should be consistent with other ground rules in your setting, for instance that you do not allow swear words or racist language.
► Sometimes children may dismiss others on the basis of their sex. Perhaps Dave is told to go away from the craft table with, 'This is just for girls. We don't want messy, noisy boys here.' You may need to step in with, 'It's not fair for you to tell Dave he can't join you' or,

depending on the fierceness of the girl's remark, perhaps, 'I think that's a hurtful thing to say to Dave. I don't think you would like to be criticised in that way.' If the girl's rejection is based on a bad experience of other boys at the craft table, or even of Dave himself, then you need to look at ways of addressing the boys' behaviour.

▶ Gentle corrections can help children to think about contradictions in what they have said; your comments can help them to learn. Perhaps a child says, 'Men don't cuddle babies, that's mummy stuff' and you counter with, 'Hold on now, I've seen your Daddy with your baby Jessica and he cuddles her a lot.'

▶ You can sometimes encourage children to look beyond their immediate experience. For instance, some children may be looking at a book and arguing about the sex of the main character. Perhaps some are saying, 'It must be a girl. Look she's got long hair.' Others may say, 'But his name's Marlon and that's a boy's name.' You could add the useful information, 'A lot of the boys in our pre-school have short hair. But boys can have longer hair and they're still boys. In this story, Marlon has his hair woven into braids.'

Sometimes children will choose to play with friends of their own sex

Children's choices in your setting

It is unlikely that the boys and girls in your setting will use the opportunities provided in the same way. There will be plenty of variation within each sex, but it is very possible that you will see some patterns. For instance, more girls may use the home corner than boys. Whereas the emphasis may be reversed for use of the outdoor tricycles or the climbing frame. It is not the case that there are no boys in the home corner nor girls on the bikes – rather that the usage of these play activities is not equal between the sexes.

RESTRICTED OPPORTUNITIES FOR LEARNING

So, if children make choices that lead them to use some parts of your setting more than others, does this matter? The simple answer is that it is not automatically a problem. You need to observe what is happening and avoid jumping to any conclusions.

Perhaps girls who explore play in the home corner have many opportunities to extend their language, to follow through imaginative themes in their play or to show a caring side in doll play. Boys whose main focus of interest is the construction equipment may be learning a great deal about planning and experimentation, size and shape and imaginative use of their final construction. Neither kind of play is restrictive in itself but might limit a child's opportunity to learn if he or she rarely ventured into the other kind of activity.

There is usually a range of different ways for children to learn particular skills and knowledge. So, an unwillingness to take part in one activity is unlikely to affect children's learning so long as other activities offer similar opportunities. A lot depends on the choices you make available in your setting and how narrowly children define their interests. Girls who decide that any kind of vigorous climbing, jumping or running is not for them, may miss out on the chance to develop confidence in their own bodies and learn considered risk-taking in physical activity. On the other hand, boys who refuse to participate in any arts, crafts or cooking may miss the chance to explore fine physical coordinations and use of tools, as well as the satisfaction of making something.

If there is a relatively firm division between girls' and boys' activities in your setting, you may also have to watch out for some areas being seen as 'just for us girls' or another area being staked out as the boys' domain. Perhaps the girls actively tell a boy to go away from the home corner or the boys will not let an interested girl join a game with the cars and lorries. Some of the following ideas could be helpful if you face this situation.

ACTIVITY

Your skills of observation will be very useful in ensuring that you avoid making assumptions about what is happening, or not happening, in your setting.

You could observe one particular area: it might be the home corner, the climbing equipment in the garden, the computer or a craft table. You can use a method called time-sampling to organise a realistic schedule of watching and listening to the children. You are unlikely to be in a position to observe all the time, so you should plan to look carefully at your focus area at regular intervals.

For example, you might decide that on Monday, Wednesday and Friday of this week, you will make an observation of the climbing area in the garden. Every ten minutes during the period that this activity is available to the children, you will write down the names of the children on or at the base of the equipment. You will also make a brief note of what the children are doing, for instance, climbing up, watching other children, calling for help and so on. At the end of your observation days, look over your information:

▶ Make a list of all the names you have and add up the number of times each child was on the frame.
▶ Do some children seem to use this equipment more than others?
▶ Are the names more one sex than another?
▶ In what ways were the children playing on the climbing equipment? Did boys and girls assume different roles, or did boys climb and girls watch?
▶ If there was a preponderance of boys (or girls), did they actively discourage children of the opposite sex?

FRIENDSHIP PATTERNS

From three to four years of age, children tend to move towards playing with peers of their own sex. This trend is not an absolute pattern; in early years settings you will see close friendships across the sexes and children who, from choice, play with both sexes. But you will also see the development of some single-sex friendships and groups who play together. This pattern can become very marked by the early years of primary school when many of the games in the playground are played in single-sex groups. Boys and girls who have close friendships can experience a great deal of teasing along the lines of 'he's your boyfriend!' or 'only cissies play with girls!'

Children should be allowed to chose their own friends, so within reason good practice is never to intervene and insist on particular patterns in play. However, a positive role for adults arises when:

▶ Children are told to go away from an activity that they have every right to join. Perhaps the group is single-sex and has staked a claim to an area or particular piece of equipment. You can step in and say, courteously but firmly, that the child can join the activity table or have a go with the trolley.

▶ Children are told to go away because of their sex, perhaps with the additional justification that 'boys are no good at ...' or 'we don't want any soppy girls'. You can disagree with the sentiment by saying, 'I think you're being unfair. I know a lot of boys who are good at ...' You can try for a compromise that will allow a child to join the existing group, but you will have to judge each situation on its merits. There is no point in insisting a child join a group, if the rest of the children are very likely to make him, or her, feel uncomfortable. Instead, you can suggest doing a different activity with the child.

▶ Do not assume the children are rejecting a child just on the basis of sex, without any other evidence, since it could be a case of natural justice. For instance, Darren may be told to go away from the dolls' tea party by a group of girls, because he has a track record of disrupting other children's play. If you listen to the children, as well as keep an observant eye on what is happening, you may realise that Darren is also told to go away by groups of boys. There is a problem to resolve here, but the focus should be Darren's difficulties in play rather than the other children's attitudes.

▶ You can join in an existing activity, or organise something yourself, to help balance any strong views based on gender stereotypes. Your presence may ease the entry of a child into a group that is mainly the opposite sex. Children are also influenced by the sex of the adult involved in an activity. So a male worker laying the tea table will communicate the clear message that men do this domestic activity, just as a female worker mending a chain on the bike gives encouragement to the girls about their options.

ACTIVITY

In the 1960s and 1970s, toy stores were quite often divided into sections for girls and sections for boys, and boxes were sometimes labelled and illustrated to reflect a firm divide between the sexes. Manufacturers and retailers are more aware now, but some gender role stereotyping remains.

On your own, or with a colleague, visit a large toy store or warehouse and make observations to explore the messages that could be given to children and their parents about the appropriateness of different play materials for the two sexes. Some suggestions for your observations follow:

▶ Look at how the toys are organised into different sections. Stores have to have some kind of organisation, but what seems to be the basis of the system?

▶ Look at the packaging of toys and play materials. If children are shown on the boxes, are they boys, girls or both? What are they doing?

▶ If you were a child, might you conclude that some play things and kinds of equipment were intended for the opposite sex? For instance, if the store has a selection of computer equipment or games, what messages are communicated about likely users?

▶ Are there different versions of the same item of play equipment? For instance, what colours are available in supposed girls' bikes and what names are given to the different types? What is available for the boys' bikes?

▶ Are there some sections that seem genuinely for both sexes? What are they?

▶ If possible, take a child who is five years or older with you on this trip (perhaps your own child, or a niece or nephew). Ask the child for his or her opinion, including which toys are supposed to be for boys or girls.

Activities within the curriculum

Conversations with children

Good practice in early years and playwork is always to give time and attention to children through conversation. Workers need to listen as well as talk, and then children will come to see you as an interesting partner in conversation.

LEARN ABOUT CHILDREN'S INTERESTS

You need to be ready to start and sustain a conversation with all the children. Adults can encourage children's language skills by showing a genuine interest in what absorbs particular children, the topics about which they want to talk. Sometimes, children want to tell you about subjects that may not interest you very much, or about which you know little. You should listen and learn from the children and, if they appear to have a narrow range of interests, you are far more likely to be able to extend that range, when you have shown respect for their current concerns.

EXPRESSING FEELINGS

It will help all the children to be able to talk about their feelings, but you may find that boys and girls have already learned that the sexes should express emotions in a different way. The more likely imbalance is that boys will have been given the message that 'big boys don't cry' or will have been criticised for behaving 'like a girl'. Girls are more likely to have been reprimanded for fierce expressions of emotion, like anger or frustration, and perhaps told 'it's not nice to shout' or 'you should be more ladylike'.

In your setting, a positive approach to behaviour should allow children the honest expression of their feelings, but within ground rules that it is unfair for anybody to unload feelings onto other people in a way that hurts physically or emotionally. Neither sex should be directed to one form of expression rather than another. Girls may benefit from learning that it is alright to be angry or frustrated with problems and that it is possible to emerge from the feelings and resolve some of the difficulties. Some boys, and indeed some girls too, try very hard not to cry and their wish should be respected; adults should never push children into crying. Children can gain from the reassurance that 'it's okay to be sad' and that a caring adult will offer comfort and practical help.

Physical games and skills

It is important that both boys and girls explore and learn a range of physical skills. Children need to feel at ease with and confident about their own bodies and need to learn how to assess risk in physical activities. The best way to learn is actually to use their growing skills of running, jumping and climbing and to experience all the physical coordinations needed for different games. Children also benefit from developing interests in pursuits that will keep them fit through childhood and into adult life.

Look at your setting and the behaviour of staff, volunteers and any parent helpers. Are the children really encouraged to choose from all those activities on offer and to learn at their own pace? The less confident children, whether girls or boys, will need encouragement to try a wide range of activities. You can suggest that a child on the climbing frame 'just climbs up to here' or offer a steadying hand to a child who needs to balance or move across a gap. Children will learn much better if they are enabled to take small risks rather than pushed to climb higher or jump further than feels comfortable to them. The same step-by-step approach is best with any physical activity that might make a child feel slightly anxious: walking along a narrow balance, swimming those first unsupported strokes or the move to a two-wheeled bike.

It is only fair that you approach children as individuals and avoid the restrictions of gender stereotypes. Some of the boys in your setting may be bold climbers and enthusiastic footballers. But other boys should not be made to feel badly about themselves because they are anxious about a climb or dislike football. Girls who become confident about their physical skills should not be restrained by adults who, without good safety reasons, say, 'Isn't that a bit high for you?' or who make remarks about 'tomboys'.

All early years centres, schools and playwork settings need a range of games involving equipment: bats and balls, large balls of different sizes, bean bags, different lengths of skipping rope and hoops. With encouragement, children will try different games. The most effective way to cross gender boundaries in physical activities is to have an involved adult who is not the 'usual' sex – a female worker playing football or a male worker skipping with a rope.

DRESS

Children's clothes nowadays are less strictly divided into boys' and girls' clothing and many girls are dressed in the kind of leisure wear that is very suitable for active play. If girls are dressed in elaborate outfits that get snagged on the slide or wear shoes that slip off when they run, you need to have a conversation with their parents. This should be a courteous exchange, with a careful explanation of why you are commenting on their daughter's clothes. Some girls may also be wearing long scarves or head covering for religious or cultural reasons and you certainly should not try to remove such items from the child. Ask parents if their daughter can temporarily tuck a scarf into her tunic so that it does not catch and tear on equipment.

ACTIVITY

Look around your setting:

▶ What kind of pictures or photographs are on the wall?
▶ What messages do the illustrations give to children or parents?
▶ Can they see *caring* men with young children as well as women?
▶ Are there female police officers as well as male, and men who are nurses as well as women?

The suppliers on page 193 will be a good source of illustrations that challenge gender stereotypes for children and adults. But you can also create unique illustrations by using photographs taken in your setting, cutting out good quality illustrations from magazines or catalogues and creating a collage. Photographs of characters from popular television programmes may also cause children to question assumptions about what men and women do.

Science and technology

All children need to develop their confidence in handling different materials and tools and in learning how to investigate and explore. Equal opportunities especially for girls, have brought about an improvement in their involvement in science and technology. Early years and playwork settings are important to ensure that this positive momentum is continued.

▶ Make sure that girls see scientific activities or a technology table as appropriate for them. An involved adult will motivate the girls, and the boys too. Ensure that both sexes are allowed to explore and find out; some adults step in more quickly to help girls, when they might find out for themselves with some verbal encouragement.

▶ Make sure that you, yourself, develop confidence in handling materials and tools, especially if you did not have much experience in this area as a child. It could be very positive for children to see you learn, experiment and persevere.

▶ Girls, or boys, who have already taken on the message that they should not make a mess, may need strong encouragement to explore. You could encourage children to investigate how objects work by taking apart old telephones, watches or other safe items, with the help of relevant tools such as screwdrivers. You can help children learn about safety too and stress that these are old bits of equipment (so that children do not go home and dismantle new items!).

▶ Look at how you could involve children in simple and safe mending or DIY activities within your setting. Gardening is also an activity in which children learn aspects of science and in which both sexes can be encouraged to take part.

Creative activities

Early years and playwork settings usually offer a wide range of play to extend children's creative skills and interests.

Music

Music and dance offer many possibilities and you can guide children to try a wide range. Notice who joins in and who stands on the sidelines. You could also watch out for unnecessary patterns such as the boys usually playing the noisier instruments like drums and the girls taking the triangles or tambourines.

ARTS AND CRAFTS

There are a tremendous range of possibilities within this area of play and learning.

▶ Painting, drawing and collage can offer children the chance of self-expression. These activities may also be an encouraging route when you want to help children to extend pretend play themes: can they portray their favourite character or even develop an illustrated story?

▶ Needlework and skills with cloth are more likely to be seen as a female occupation. If boys are reluctant to join a table with these activities, then a male worker or volunteer can be a boost to their involvement. It is also useful if children see workers using such skills in a practical way. For instance, a male or female worker might be sewing buttons back on or mending some of the dressing-up clothes.

▶ Working with wood and the relevant tools may, in contrast, be seen more as a male preserve. Again, an involved adult can help to balance up the use of the activity between the sexes. Your presentation of this activity (and others) may be strengthened with illustrations and photos of children and adults who have crossed the gender line and are enjoying learning new skills.

▶ Cooking activities combine creative, mathematical, literacy and scientific skills (of measuring, blending and how substances change with the application of heat). Highlight these different sides of what children may feel is a boring domestic activity and you may bring in more children and also hook the attention of boys who resist a seemingly more female occupation. There are now also plenty of male chefs on television, so you should be able to create a collage that shows men cooking as well as women.

ACTIVITY

Do you ever organise a play activity just for the girls or just for the boys? If you feel that either sex is being excluded or is less confident to join a particular activity, then a single-sex focus may help.

▶ It is important to plan such a session and to be able to explain your reasons to children or parents.

▶ Perhaps you can arrange a session on the climbing equipment or with the construction materials for girls who seem daunted by the more

active boys. Or a cooking time may be beneficial for boys who are interested but have been discouraged by more adept or disdainful girls.
▶ Make sure that single sex sessions even up across boys and girls. And ask the children what they think about the chance to pursue an activity with just their own sex.

Pretend play

DOLLS AND PLAY PEOPLE

The messages are strong that dolls are girls' toys, but some boys may still express an interest when there is a good range of dolls, including boy dolls as well as girl dolls. Perhaps one of the boys in your group has a new baby sister or brother – can he demonstrate how to hold a little baby by using a baby doll? Some of the suppliers on page 193 have a wide range of dolls of both sexes, sometimes anatomically correct, as well as reflecting a range of ethnic groups.

Boys may back away from dolls but still want to use a set of play people who fit with some of the different construction sets or with the settings such as a farm or a castle.

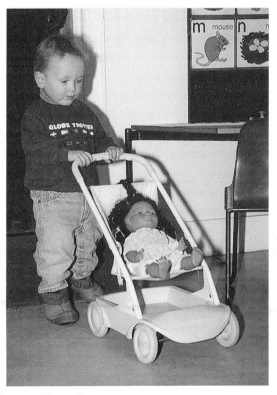

Dolls and other play materials are for everyone

The Home Corner

The quieter area known in most early years settings as 'the home corner' can, of course, become other venues such as a shop, a doctor's surgery or a hairdressing salon. Some play themes may be more attractive to some children than others, so it is wise to make changes from time to time. All the children deserve a chance in the home corner and you may need to watch that boys are not ordered away by the girls – or bossed about in the home setting and given very restrictive roles. Children may become irritated if adults intervene regularly in their pretend play in this area, so you may choose to raise those issues at another time.

Children's play will reflect their experience to date, much of it from their family life. So, it is important to show respect for their views, even when you do not agree. For instance, a group of girls may be pretend cooking and two boys sitting waiting to be served. Carline's statement that 'men can't cook' might be met with, 'Some men can't cook but I know a lot who can. How about, next time David does the cooking and you put your feet up?'

Dressing-Up Clothes

Some dressing-up boxes are weighted towards female clothing, which perhaps reflects the source of free clothing for this activity. Yet, boys may find less to attract their attention. You can make sure that your range of hats or wigs definitely has items for males as well as females. A range of work-related uniforms and hats will add possibilities for all the children (a fire fighter, bus conductor, police officer, doctor or nurse). Try to add some costumes to your collection or items for creating a super hero or heroine outfit, knight's armour or astronaut's suit.

Parents do not usually mind their daughters dressing up in male attire, but some are genuinely anxious that letting their sons dress up in female clothing will turn the boys into gay men or transvestites. It is necessary to respect parents' concerns, while reassuring them that dressing up in a feather boa or a long wig will not affect their son's future sexual orientation. Perhaps comparing the activity to the English cultural tradition of pantomime dames will help. (Male transvestites are often heterosexual, but this may not be much comfort to a parent with very traditional views.) Adult men who cross-dress sometimes recall how this preference started in childhood. However, the wish to dress up or experiment with make-up seems to have been present from a young age and was not caused by access to a dressing-up box.

The Media and Play

You need a balanced approach towards television programmes or films that absorb children and whose themes may enter their pretend play. It is understandable to have reservations about the forceful marketing of toys linked with television series and films for children. But adults need to show respect for children's interests, as well as looking for ways to re-direct pretend play that has become more violent than vigorous.

▶ Avoid being dismissive about programmes that children clearly enjoy and which fuel imaginative play. How would you feel if children were rude about your favourite programmes or videos?

▶ Be ready to have a conversation about the programme – which means taking the opportunity to watch at least a couple of episodes. Children who do not hold long conversations about other topics may well use their language to talk about favourite characters and plots.

▶ Watch any pretend play with an open mind. It may look aggressive, but is it really? Are children being hurt or intimidated, or is the lively activity fuelled by excitement? Adults have to be careful about imposing themes on children's fantasy play and making assumptions about what is 'playing properly'.

▶ Children's fantasy play is often based on themes that absorb them from television and films, as well as favourite story books. If you do not like the themes, what might you do that is still respectful of children's enthusiasm? You could encourage children to explore their interest through other forms: draw a picture, make up an episode for a simple drama session, draw and write up an episode, perhaps with help.

▶ Adults owe it to children (and I hear more reservations about boys and their favourite programmes) to reflect on what absorbs children and not just offer a thoughtless reaction of 'it's rubbish!' Think about what attracts children (girls as well as boys) to the idea of super heroes and heroines.

Boys' Games?

Observation of children in early years settings or schools shows some differences between the preferred play of boys and girls. Boys, on average, engage in more rough and tumble than girls and their games more often develop an element of play fighting. The concerned reaction of mainly female staff teams has often led to attempts to redirect the boys' energy into other forms of play and sometimes to ban certain games.

Any area of good practice has to be open to review and during the 1990s there was much rethinking about boys' physical games and to what extent they really posed problems. It is not women's fault that they may be less in tune with boys' play, and females certainly have not been actively keeping men out of early years settings or primary schools. But, it is far from ideal if any children, in this case the boys, experience a consistently negative attitude from adults towards the play activities that they find the most exciting, entertaining or important. Current thinking about boys' games includes the following:

▶ A proper consideration of whether the boys' games really are too noisy or rough. Can workers step aside from an outright ban and talk over with the boys where or when they play the games?

▶ Some ground rules. Perhaps there is no wrestling in the home corner, super hero pretend play happens out in the garden or you draw the line at weapons.

▶ Consideration of the fact that boys react better to genuine adult interest in the characters and plots of their pretend play, than to complaints about the disruptive nature of their imaginary games. The themes and roles may then be extended rather than this kind of play retreating to the less obvious areas of your setting. On the other hand, you may find that a game you had mentally dismissed as simple aggression, has complex themes and characters that the boys develop from day to day.

▶ Questioning how far you can let play fighting go before you intervene. Workers are understandably concerned about children getting hurt. However, few play fights appear to turn into genuine aggressive attacks and children, girls as well as boys, seem well able to tell the difference. Boys seem to use physical rough and tumble as one way to form and sustain friendships.

ACTIVITY

Boys deserve space and respect for their consuming interests just as girls do.

▶ If you are considering a ban on a largely boys' activity, think about an activity that equally absorbs some of the girls. Do you try to redirect their interest or limit their chosen game? If not, then what makes the girls' play more acceptable to you?

▶ If you are an all-female staff team, then spend some time exploring a male perspective, which may be different. You might talk with some of the fathers or with male friends or partners. Express your concerns but listen properly to their viewpoint.

Books and literacy

CHOICE OF BOOKS

There is now a wide choice of books which show men and women, boys and girls in a range of situations, roles and activities. A balanced selection of books offers children a range of images:

▶ Women and girls will not always be in the caring, domestic or follower role. Sometimes girls will be the leader of a group, a heroine or a strong character in a story. There is absolutely nothing the matter with stories that feature caring mothers or girls absorbed in traditional female activities, so long as these are not the only images available to the children.

▶ Men and boys can be strong, leaders and explorers. But some stories need to show males who follow, consult or work alongside females. Male characters should show a range of emotions: caring, anxiety, curiosity and other feelings – certainly not all macho aggression and competitiveness.

▶ Check that your books have a wide range of topics. Once children start to read, girls seem to be generally more open about the books they choose to read. They are more likely than boys to cross the line and read 'boys' books' than the boys are likely to read books that are clearly pitched towards girls.

T O   T H I N K   A B O U T

Girls are not usually put off a book by a male main character but the reverse happens more often: boys are less interested in a book with a heroine. Why do you think this happens? Share and discuss your thoughts with colleagues, fellow-students or friends outside your profession – ideally male as well as female.

▶ When you chose books, you need to look out for an absorbing story line, as well as other features. Children's attention will not be held by a weak plot, however well-intentioned the author may be about equal opportunities. It is far more effective to *show* through the story line that children or adults can step out of gender stereotypes, than to have a narrator or characters who simply *tell* children that there are many possibilities.

▶ Look at the illustrations in books as well as reading the story. What images do the pictures communicate? Take a close look also at any illustrations in non-fiction information books: are there girls featured in a science book or boys shown caring for animals in a book about pets?

BOYS AND LITERACY

During the 1990s, there was a growing awareness that too many boys were deciding at an early age that books, school work and study were not for them. In addition, more boys than girls have dyslexia, a specific learning disability that affects reading and writing. However, many of the boys turning away from literacy skills are not dyslexic. They have learned the basics of reading, but see little point in using and extending their skills. Some older boys and young men reject books and study as not being a masculine activity. Their future prospects look grim in a world with considerably less semi-skilled work than was available for past generations.

Practical ideas to address this potential problem can be equally useful for young girls who have not warmed to books:

▶ Make sure that the reading, and browsing, material for children is taken from a wide range of sources. Many children like story books, but some are more attracted to books that are informative about subjects, especially for when they are looking on their own.

▶ You might buy or borrow from the library some of the following: books about how machines work, practical science, sharks or dinosaurs, animals, space travel, sports, picture dictionaries or books about art and craft (perhaps linked with television programmes that children enjoy). Publishers such as Dorling Kindersley or Usborne have a very wide selection of information books.

▶ Avoid drawing hard boundaries around what is or is not 'proper' reading matter. Some children are keen on joke books, comic style books and stories that feature super heroes or other characters from television or film. You may still retain your views about a television or film character, but do not dismiss the reading source out of hand.

ACTIVITY

Children's general knowledge and their wish to know more is often fuelled by books that are attractive to the young browser: good photographs or clear sketches and simple text.

▶ Over several weeks, keep a note of those books that seem to be most used by the girls and boys in your setting.

▶ If you can organise a library trip, then observe which books the children look at or want to take out on loan.

Some children become passionately interested in stories and all kinds of books. Boys and girls who have not developed such enthusiasm may be drawn to other kinds of written material, which also gives the message that literacy skills are valuable in everyday life. Avoid seeing books as material that must stay in the book corner.

▶ Mail order catalogues or telephone directories could be placed in the home corner.
▶ There can be illustrated instructions and suggestions for building models on the construction table or area.
▶ Art and craft books or magazines with good quality illustrations can inspire creative work.
▶ Counting books, puzzle and pattern books could be placed close to mathematical activities.
▶ A well illustrated recipe book could guide and provide ideas for cooking activities. You can also compile your own book from recipes that you and the children try.

MALE ROLE MODELS

The staff in early years settings and early primary school are mainly female. One of the consequences of this imbalance is that some boys swiftly come to the conclusion that books and other forms of school work are 'girly'. Young boys who have a positive male role model at home are far less likely to be deflected from school achievement. Fathers who read to their children and

All children need equal access to current technology

who show pleasure in books and school work are likely to encourage their sons along the same route, as well as communicating to their daughters that fathers care about books. An older brother, liked uncle or other male relative could offer the same kind of role model and support. But this has to be an active involvement; the men have to show that they really value literacy and study.

Some British primary schools have become sufficiently concerned about boys' rejection of books and study that they have asked fathers to volunteer a couple of hours each week to come into school and hear boys read. Saying that boys need men is not a criticism of the value of women. Boys and girls can learn much from adults of both sexes. But children will mainly look towards the adults of their own sex for the messages about what a real grown up person does and thinks, and what they do not do.

ACTIVITY

If your staff team is all female, it is worth exploring whether fathers or grandfathers would give some time to boost a male interest in literacy. This initiative needs to be organised in a positive way.

▶   It is important that male volunteers are seen to respect the lead and authority of a female worker. It will be very unhelpful if the volunteers appear to take over a group or act in any way that undermines the female staff.
▶   Boys who are perhaps already developing a macho approach to females will benefit from seeing an adult male relate positively to a woman who is responsible for the group. Boys can see the volunteer listen to what a female worker suggests, perhaps asking, 'What would you like me to do?' or 'Where would you like me to start today?'
▶   When volunteers are comfortable in the setting, you could take some photographs of men and women reading with children and create a display.

Relationships between the adults

A very female profession

Women far outnumber men on the staff teams of early years settings. Only about 1% of nursery nurses are men. Multi-disciplinary centres which draw their staff from a wider range of professions are more likely to have male staff. Playwork settings, such as after-school clubs, have relatively more men because of their different tradition and links with youth work. Primary schools have predominantly female staff teams. In 1997, male teachers accounted for only 17% of teachers of children under eight, although they held 47% of the nursery and primary headships. The Teacher Training Agency forecast that, if the decline continues, then there will be no male teachers in primary schools by 2010.

The main reason why women predominate in work with young children is almost certainly the powerful social attitudes that care and education of young children is naturally a female occupation. This bias has been linked with a history of low pay and limited career prospects, although this situation has improved somewhat in recent decades. There is nothing the matter with women caring for children, so long as this occupation is properly valued, which too often is not the case.

Mixed staff teams

Children come in two sexes, as do adults, and all children need to be able to relate positively to each sex. A mixed staff group, or a mainly female group supplemented by regular male volunteers, can be the most effective way of opening up possibilities for all the children. Books, posters or conversations are useful ways of shaking strong views about gender stereotypes. But real people acting in a flexible way is one of the most effective ways to challenge any stereotype.

▶ Any mixed team needs to monitor how the daily tasks are being delegated within the team. Males and females need to take both the tasks that are, and are not, seen as natural for their sex.

▶ Children need to observe female workers who make decisions within a mixed sex team, who show physical confidence and considered risk taking. Women may be competent at cooking and crafts, but they are also enthusiastic about numbers or scientific investigation in the nursery.

▶ Male workers may be adept at the wood working table or building in the garden, although they may not be confident in these crafts, of course. Male workers can show their caring side, that men can consult with others and admit that they are unsure or still learning. A rounded male worker can show his skills with a hurt child who needs comfort, have a quiet conversation, as well as show physical dexterity at football.

▶ Workers of both sexes can be seen by children to listen to each other, consult and learn from one another and on occasion to defer to the opinion of a colleague of the opposite sex, without the implication that one sex is usually right and the other wrong.

BEHAVIOUR WITHIN THE TEAM

Female workers must be ready to address their own assumptions and attitudes about males: as colleagues and male carers in the home. I have heard early years workers complain about the lack of men in the profession and then soon afterwards make snide remarks about a male carer like, 'He'll make someone a lovely wife one day.' The head of centre and senior staff are responsible for ensuring that teams talk through the issues in an open way. Everyone has some assumptions and expectations that could disrupt smooth team work. It is better to explore these honestly than to pretend that all the issues about male colleagues are practical. There is more to discuss than whether male and female workers are prepared to share the same set of staff toilets.

An existing team has to make male workers or volunteers welcome. It is a considered balance between welcoming Steve as a new colleague who has to settle in like anyone else, and acknowledging the unusual experience of any person joining a profession which is dominated by the opposite sex. Some practical thoughts follow:

▶ Listen to male colleagues as much as to other team members. But do not ask or expect them to speak up on a regular basis as a man, more than as a colleague. If a male colleague appears to dominate discussion, then the imbalance should be handled in the same way as with any more outspoken team member. A head of centre needs to ensure that female workers are not deferring to a male colleague and then complaining later that he has taken over the discussion.

▶ A male colleague may be able to give a fresh perspective, because he is man, but he should not be expected to represent the whole male sex. (Just as a colleague of a different ethnic group to the rest of the team should not be pushed into a demanding expert role all the time.) Nor should a male worker be required to defend or explain the behaviour of other people, just because they are men.

▶ Be aware of staff room conversation. A previously all-female group may have developed bad habits of complaining about men in general. It is not fair behaviour to make highly critical remarks about men and then say to a male colleague 'but you're different'. It would not be acceptable to make comments like this to a black colleague, so it is not reasonable when he is a man.

▶ If there is more than one male worker in a team, let them talk together without a fuss. Some female workers react with 'now they're ganging up', when they would not say the same about two female workers. (Incidentally, females in predominantly male occupations report the same kind of frustrating experience.)

▶ Anyone in the minority in a profession can benefit from an appropriate professional network and men in child care have developed groups for mutual support. (See page 73 for details.)

Male colleagues should cover the same range of responsibilities as the female team members. Male workers should not be expected to take over the physically more active boys, nor to be the main one to discipline. Some individual boys may respond better to a male figure and to develop this would be a proper reaction of the team to the result of a child's experience and temperament. A male worker may be invaluable in showing this child that maleness can co-exist with respect for others and especially for females. Discipline must also be an issue for all workers. A team will have to deal sensitively with any parent who homes in on the one or two male workers with the expectation that they will discipline the children.

There may be some activities that become the main responsibility of a male worker, but the pattern should not be allowed to slip into gender stereotyping. Open and honest discussion amongst the team will be crucial. Ask yourselves whether is it wise that a man has moved into taking the more physical activities. What are your reasons for letting this happen and why is a female worker not taking a turn? Do not blame each other, rather look at what seems to be happening. Consider the reasons and discuss whether they are valid. What could you do in the future? Acknowlege that the adults in the staff team are learning as much as the children and finding new ways to tackle old habits.

Child Protection Issues

Increased awareness of child abuse has complicated the issues around male workers with children. Some teams and local authorities have developed rules limiting the daily responsibilities of male workers and some are resistant to employing men at all. Unfortunately such an approach is not an effective method of child protection and places severe limits on children's learning experiences.

A major misunderstanding in this area comes from the inaccurate claim that 'most abusers are male'. Men predominate in sexual abuse but not in physical abuse, neglect or emotional abuse of children. (Some sexual abuse is also perpetrated by females.) Women can be cruel to children and neglectful of their needs, so banning men is no way to deal with child protection in early years. All settings need clear procedures for taking on paid workers and volunteers and a working atmosphere in which children, parents and workers feel able to raise any concerns.

Partnership with parents

Conversation and Explanation

As with any aspect of good practice in your setting, you should be ready to talk with parents about what you do and why. For instance, parents may need to know that:

▶ You are opening opportunities for all children, rather than shutting them down. You would like girls and boys to feel able to learn a range of skills. You no more stop girls doing needlework than you insist that they play football.

▶ Equal opportunities on gender are not only focused on the girls, you are all equally alert to boys' outlook and learning.

▶ Children develop their social attitudes early. The nursery or pre-school is a good place to ensure that children do not restrict their own opportunities or feel bad about themselves because they have non-traditional interests.

Some parents will share your views and want to support the work in the setting. Some may appreciate a chance to express their frustrations from within the family, because they have been trying to extend a son or daughter's interests, against opposition from a partner or relative. Some will disagree for reasons related to cultural or religious traditions and some of these parents will be white British, certainly not all from minority ethnic groups.

TO THINK ABOUT

Read through the following examples and consider how you might reply if a parent said this to you. You could compare ideas with a colleague or fellow student.

1 'It says in your brochure something about equal opportunities and gender. What exactly does that mean?'

2 'I don't want you to let my son do this needlework stuff. He's a boy; he should be playing with cars and trains, not doing embroidery. Are you trying to turn them into wimps?'

3 'I was pleased that you have all the climbing equipment but my mother has been going on, since she picked Lisa up last week. Mum has a thing about little girls falling onto their privates; she wouldn't let me climb when I was a child. What do you think about it, is it risky?'

4 'I know all this gender stuff is very politically correct – very feminist. But I think you should keep politics out of the nursery. They're children and you're trying to brainwash them.'

5 'I don't really mind about Jon playing in your home corner with the dolls, because he's very young still. But his Dad's really uncomfortable about it. What happens when he's older, will you do football and things with him?'

6 'I agree that children learn very young. But they should be learning what will help them when they are grown up. And that means learning how to behave like a proper young lady or young man.'

The families of children who attend your setting may be a valuable resource to complement the skills of your team. Perhaps some parents have skills, interests or occupations which are less usual for their sex. Even when parents cannot help out as a regular volunteer, they may be pleased to visit or they may have access to positive illustrations that could be used in the setting.

MALE CARERS

Even though your team may be mainly or completely female, the parents who bring and pick up children may include more men. Early years workers need to be aware of their own attitudes and offer respect for male carers, such as fathers. Watch out that you do not assume that this is a temporary arrangement and ask when the child's mother will be coming. Male carers may be lone parents or may be the primary carer in a two parent family. Alternatively some families organise their time so that both parents share in taking children to and from a nursery or school.

You should communicate directly with the parent in front of you and not use fathers simply as a channel for sending messages back to the child's mother. When both parents come, do not address all your remarks to the mother or always ask her questions about health or routine. Some fathers may be more comfortable talking with a male worker, if there is that option, but not necessarily. Certainly fathers should not be directed towards a male worker, any more than black parents should be pushed into conversation with a black member of staff.

DIFFERENT KINDS OF FAMILIES

There will undoubtedly be some diversity in the families who attend your setting. You will have some children being raised by their birth parents. But some will be cared for by one parent – a mother or father – because the other parent has left the home or has died. Some families will be formed by new relationships and stepparents and stepsiblings will be part of the family. Some children may have been adopted or are in a long term foster placement.

Gay and lesbian parents are a group with a great deal of individual variation, just like any social group of people. They may feel understandably under pressure or scrutiny about their sexuality and the negative reaction of many people to their raising children. So you may not necessarily know that an individual parent is gay or lesbian.

The parents will want to talk to you about the wide range of issues that affect children and which they share with other fellow parents. They will want you to relate to them in their social role as parent to their children. Their sexuality may not arise as an issue, any more than your own sexual orientation or whether you have a current partner.

Many gay and lesbian parents had their children while they were in a previous heterosexual relationship. Some make choices to become a parent while they are in a gay or lesbian relationship. Gay and lesbian parents, just like many other parents, have the experience of managing a relationship with the child's biological parent, with whom they are no longer living. Gay fathers will probably not be the custodial parent but may, like other committed fathers, attend functions at your setting or take turns with the child's mother to bring or pick up his child(ren).

Research is still limited on gay and lesbian households with children, but the indications are consistent so far. Children do not seem to be confused about their own sex or in finding an appropriate gender identity; certainly there is no reason to assume that their emotional development is affected. Children's emotional stability and well being seems to depend on how they are treated by adults, not those adults' sexual orientation. Living in a gay or lesbian family does not appear to push children's sexuality one way or another. The children are no more likely to grow up gay or lesbian, than children in heterosexual households.

If you are uncertain how to deal with children's comments or questions, then talk with the parents involved. They will have experience and preferences about how their family is described. The parents could be valuable in helping you decide how best to reply when one child says to another, 'You can't have two Mummies' or asks, 'Is Mike your Daddy's lodger?' Children can be made unhappy or feel isolated if their family situation is met with hostility or offensive amusement. In an unwelcoming local community children may also feel that they have to be secretive about their family and children are rarely comfortable keeping secrets that prevent them talking openly about their life and what is important to them.

Further resources

Books

Blatchford, Peter and Sharp, Sonia (eds) (1994) *Breaktime and the School: understanding and changing playground behaviour* (Routledge)
Thoughtful approach to what is often the forgotten area of children's school experience.

Browne, Naima and France, Pauline '*Only Cissies Wear Dresses*' – *a look at sexist talk in the nursery* in Weiner, Gaby (ed) (1985) *Just a Bunch of Girls: feminist approaches to schooling* (Open University Press)
Most of Weiner's book focuses on late primary and secondary school. But this chapter is a description of what adults say to children of nursery age and the issues that arise.

Browne, Naima and France, Pauline (eds) (1986) *Untying the Apron Strings: anti-sexist provision for the under-fives* (Open University Press)
General background on the issues in anti-sexist practice for early years.

De'Ath, Erica (1991) *Changing Families: a guide for early years workers* (National Early Years Network, Starting Points Series no. 10)
A practical booklet broadening assumptions about how families may be composed and the social changes in family structure.

Equality Learning Centre (1996) *Boys Reading and Writing* and *Passionate About Print*.
Two practical leaflets about encouraging literacy, especially counteracting the possibility that boys will feel the activity is not for them.

Equal Opportunities Commission (1992) *An Equal Start: guidelines on equal treatment for the under-eights* (EOC)
The background to equal opportunities on gender and possibilities within the national curriculum.

Jensen, Jytte Juul (1995) *Men as Workers in Childcare Services* (European Commission Network on Childcare)
Discussion of the issues involved in men working with young children – a perspective from different European countries.

Hyder, Tina and Kenway, Penny (1995) *An Equal Future: a guide to anti-sexist practice in the early years* (National Early Years Network, Starting Points Series no. 20)
Practical booklet about underlying issues and good practice.

Kropp, Paul and Cooling, Wendy (1995) *The Reading Solution: making your child a reader for life* (Penguin)

Practical suggestions for encouraging children to use their literacy skills in study and reading for pleasure.

Lindon, Jennie (1998) *Child Protection and Early Years Work* (Hodder and Stoughton)
An explanation of good practice in the early years setting, including discussion of issues raised by the employment of male workers. Written particularly with students and practitioners in mind.

Melville, Sandra (1994) *Gender Matters: a guide to gender issues and children's play* (Playboard)
Practical ideas for equal opportunities practice in early years and playwork settings.

Miedzian, Myriam (1992) *Boys Will be Boys – breaking the link between masculinity and violence* (Virago)
Thought-provoking discussion about the pressures on boys and young men, and of social attitudes that value aggression.

Paley, Vivian Gussin (1984) *Boys and Girls: superheroes in the doll corner* (University of Chicago Press)
Description of Paley's own nursery, the play she observed and her reflections on what she saw and heard.

Pipher, Mary (1994) *Reviving Ophelia: saving the selves of adolescent girls* (Vermilion)
A sensitive book about the pressures that lead adolescent girls to undervalue themselves.

Ruxton, Sandy (1992) *What's He Doing at the Family Centre: the dilemmas of men who care for children* (National Children's Home Research Report)
Discussion and personal examples of the position of men who work in centres for young children.

Sharpe, Sue (1976) *Just like a girl: how girls learn to be women* (Penguin)
Much of this book still rings true for the current generation as for when it was first published.

Organisations

Equal Opportunities Commission, Overseas House, Quay Street, Manchester M3 3HN Tel: 0161 833 9244
The EOC is specifically responsible for monitoring the legislation on equal opportunities.

European Commission Network on Childcare, Network Coordinator, Peter Moss, Thomas Coram Research Unit, 27/28 Woburn Square, London WC1H 0AA Tel: 0171 612 6957
The Network's full title describes the focus of the work: European

Commission Network on Childcare and Other Measures to Reconcile Employment and Family Responsibilities for Women and Men. The network has published several reports on male workers in early years.

Men Who Care c/o Early Childhood Project, Royal York Buildings, Old Steine, Brighton, Sussex BN1 1NH Tel: 01273 732002
A network for men in the early years and caring professions. They have meetings and a newsletter.

Other organisations are concerned about equal opportunities on gender as well as other aspects of good practice. You will find suggestions in the more general list from page 192.

3

Diversity in ethnic group and cultural tradition

Use of terms and language

There are no easy answers as to how to describe people when you are talking about groups rather than known individuals. A practical way forward is to become aware of the meaning of words and phrases and how they may reflect people's attitudes.

▶ **Race**: There is no scientific basis for the concept of 'race'. Genetic research has consistently shown a high level of variation within any of the groupings that have been investigated. You can say that we are all of mixed racial origins but it is impossible to assign people to a single 'race'.

▶ **Racism**: A set of attitudes, actions and practice that subordinates a group of people because of their skin colour, culture or ethnic group. Racist beliefs are used to justify racial discrimination.

▶ **Racial discrimination**: The denial or restriction of opportunities to individuals from the defined group.

▶ **Institutional racism:** Describes how attitudes can shape the way in which organisations operate.

▶ **Ethnic**: This word is an adjective used to describe a national or cultural identity. Everyone has their own source of ethnicity; all people have their own ethnic origins. So individuals of Celtic origin, Gaelic or Scandinavian are an ethnic group just as much as people of Thai, Moroccan or Bangladeshi origin.

▶ **Minority ethnic:** An ethnic group that has a relatively small total number of individuals, in comparison with the total population, but which might comprise most of the local population in a particular geographical area.

▶ **Ethnocentric**: Describes an outlook based very firmly in individuals' own perspective, with the strong belief that their own group and traditions are superior to those of others. This outlook is sometimes called **cultural racism**.

▶ **Culture**: Describes the particular patterns of behaviour and associated beliefs which are shared by the individuals within a given group. Not all individuals will necessarily follow these patterns in exactly the same way.

Attitudes, ideas and learning

A history of ethnic diversity

Current ethnic diversity in Britain is not just the result of population movements in the second half of the twentieth century. The origins of many white British families are far from 100% English; many will have mixed European and Celtic or Gaelic origins, if nothing else. Britain was a sea-faring nation and had many thriving ports around the country. Sailors and visitors from many other countries landed and often stayed. Most of these arrivals were men, they married local women and over the generations their ethnic origins became less and less obvious in their descendants. It is an ironic thought that a proportion of racist demonstrators in areas like the East End of London will have black ancestors, if their family has been in the area for generations. Traces of the previous black population are sometimes left in names, for instance in the West Country surname of 'Blackmore' – allegedly a reference to North African Moors and Blackamoors.

The past in the present

The present for any society is shaped in many ways by what has happened in the past. In previous centuries, Britain was a dominant force in the world, in competition with other European nations. Britain was actively involved in the slave trade, when considerable numbers of Africans were forcibly taken across the Atlantic to the Caribbean and what later became the United States. The wish to secure trade and further desire for expansion led to the colonisation of large and small countries around the world to form what became known as the British Empire.

At the time of these events, and for many years afterwards, the prevailing view was that British activities were justified for economic reasons and that the colonised peoples benefited from a civilising influence. The dominant attitude was that British culture, religious beliefs, education and social systems were superior and that indigenous peoples were definitely inferior, the only question being just how 'primitive' or 'uncivilised'. Such views became an integral part of British culture and were reflected in material for children, for instance within their school textbooks.

Books from the first decades of the twentieth century present the glory of the British Empire. But in the 1960s and 1970s the emphasis was still often on the civilising effect of the British presence, with very little respect for other traditions, or even a recognition that the colonised countries had a real culture. The slave trade, although not justified completely, was often presented as an unfortunate economic necessity.

So generations of children grew up with a conviction that the white British way of life was not only the best, but had brought light into the darkness (a very common image) of primitive countries. A liberal outlook was that people from the African or Indian continent or the Caribbean could be educated and therefore be made 'more like us'. An overtly racist outlook was that non-white peoples were inherently inferior and always would be, and were not welcome as residents in Britain. The legacy of history has been that black residents of Britain have frequently met with prejudiced attitudes and active discrimination. By the 1970s and onwards, enough people (white as well as black) felt strongly that the situation was completely unacceptable and that positive action had to be taken, through legislation and direct work on people's attitudes in action.

INSTITUTIONAL RACISM

Racist attitudes influenced the way that people worked. Within organisations, systems and procedures have to be developed in the first place by individuals. Those people may have been explicitly racist, but were just as likely to have made decisions on the basis of assumptions that they simply never questioned or checked.

Once systems are in place that operate in a discriminatory way, they give support to individuals who are openly racist and encourage a sense of inertia for those who are much less racist in outlook or intention. It is hard work to challenge a set of procedures that carry the weight of tradition and are presented as normal. In a similar way, organisations can have systems with consequences that are sexist, even when the individuals following the procedures can honestly say that they did not personally intend this result.

A BROAD VIEW

In equal opportunities and ethnic group, a considerable emphasis has understandably been placed on racist attitudes held by white people about black ethnic groups. However, developing views about good practice have properly tried to avoid this simplistic perspective that overlooks inequalities or offensive attitudes about other groups. For instance, anti-semitism has a long history in

Britain, as well as in other European countries. Non-English but British ethnic groups, such as the Welsh or Scots, can also look back on a history of oppression of their culture and language. It is very usual now, for instance, to hear a wide range of accents on the television or radio. But generations of people with regional accents deliberately lost their Irish, Cornish or other accents to increase acceptance and avoid offensive remarks presented as jokes.

What is normal?

Children tend to assume that their life is an accurate reflection of the lives of most other people. So, if they have grandparents living with their family, they are surprised to learn that a friend does not. Until they learn more, they may assume that, because they have a baby sister, anyone else's new baby will also be a little girl. Children gradually learn about the variety within their world, but relatively narrow horizons can remain with them into adulthood unless they are stimulated to think more broadly.

What you know seems normal to you – the natural or obvious way of organising a life or raising children. Different ways may seem odd, exotic or suspect. The consequence of this outlook can be the conviction that, 'I talk normally, people from other parts of the country have a strong accent' or, 'I bring up my children the way I was raised; I don't have a cultural tradition.' But cultural traditions are not just something that happen to other people; everyone has a cultural background and everyone has an ethnic group to which they belong.

Some aspects of culture are rooted in religious beliefs which have shaped the traditions of a given society or social group. Some patterns of behaviour can therefore persist, even when individuals are not active followers of a particular religious faith. Cultural traditions can affect everyday behaviour as well as influence the details of special occasions or festivals. Diet and style of eating, habits, forms of spoken and non-verbal communication can all be shaped by cultural traditions.

OPENNESS OR ETHNOCENTRISM?

A meeting of traditions can lead to surprise or interest. The feelings may be more of uneasiness and uncertainty, followed by adjustment. Alternatively, the difference in culture may be taken as a reason to reject the other group and take up an ethnocentric outlook.

Individuals who persist in this kind of selective perception are currently unable, or unwilling, to acknowledge that other traditions, practices and values could be worthy of respect. Those with an ethnocentric outlook insist on taking their own traditions as the measure of what is normal and probably superior. An ethnocentric approach can be part of a restricted view within early years work, when workers would perhaps object to being described as racist.

Misuse of the word 'ethnic' can highlight narrow or dismissive views of cultures other than that of the person speaking. The word is sometimes used wrongly as a noun and individuals are referred to as 'an ethnic' or a group as 'ethnics'. In some instances the term is used effectively to mean exotic. For example, 'ethnic' is being misused when it is applied to tandoori chicken but not to steak and kidney pie, or to Indian dances but not to English country dancing. Some catalogues for children's play materials perpetuate the idea that there is 'our' culture and there are other cultures. For instance, in one, otherwise good quality, catalogue I noticed that the single black glove puppet out of a choice of ten was called 'Ethnic Girl'.

Early learning

Young children do not automatically assume that skin colour or visible cultural differences mean that people are more or less worthy. However, children who are exposed to racist attitudes and actions soon use what they have heard, or the behaviour they have watched, to build a negative image associated with a different skin colour, or with other indicators of ethnic origin or cultural difference.

Prejudice has an impact on how children feel about themselves, as well as their attitude towards others. Those children who are part of the dominant ethnic or cultural group may boost their sense of self-worth by disparaging others. Their pride in their own group, and in themselves as a member of that group, may be supported largely by feelings of superiority or by ridiculing others. The racist views learned by some children will gain a stronger hold, if responsible adults do not counteract the dismissive sense of arrogance.

The children, who are part of the group to which the prejudice is directed, are soon fully aware of this rejection. They are at risk of low self-esteem and doubts about their own worth. Research has established that some young black children – as young as four and five years – that have encountered sufficiently racist beliefs, expressed by others, have actively said that they would prefer to be white. Strong and supportive adults can help children, but only through directly challenging the racist attitudes which attack children's confidence, and through continued support of children's sense of their own worth and self-esteem.

ACTIVITY

Workers in early years, playwork or school settings will sometimes express views about equal opportunities, in relation to ethnic group and culture, that have not been carefully considered or which are revealing of more prejudiced attitudes. Think about the following comments and discuss them with colleagues or fellow students. You may like to return to this activity when you have read more of the chapter.

▶ What are the unspoken assumptions in what people have said?
▶ In what ways are they misunderstanding what is meant by equal opportunities?
▶ What could be a first step in tackling the views expressed?

1 'I don't see why we have to have all this race stuff. It's not like we're living in an inner city area. Thank goodness we don't have those sort of problems around here.'
2 'But the families come to this country because they want an English way of life and they want their children to be English. They don't want us to do all these different cultures.'
3 'People should act normally like we do. You know that saying, "When in Rome, act as the Romans do". Anyway children don't like to stand out; they want to merge in with everyone else.'
4 'We were here first. It's our country, they should fit in with us. Why should we have to change everything to fit in with them?'
5 'We've done our multicultural week, perhaps now we'll be left in peace to get on with the real work.'
6 'But if we do all these special projects for the ethnic children, the white children will feel horribly left out, they'll think we're not interested in them at all.'

Equal opportunities in the curriculum

Working in mainly white areas

Although some areas of Britain show very little evidence of ethnic diversity, especially if the focus is on skin colour, the national, cultural and religious origins of local families may have many sources of diversity. However, this fact is not immediately obvious if the majority of the population are white. Several issues arise from this daily experience of apparent non-diversity.

There will be some diversity in any parent group, although this is not always obvious

CHILDREN'S LEARNING

Some people hold the view that equal opportunities in connection with ethnic group and cultural tradition are only relevant in so far as differences can be seen locally. Undoubtedly some of the emphasis in equal opportunities is that individual children can see themselves in the play materials and curriculum of their setting. So, in one way the composition of the local population is important. But another goal in any setting should be to extend children's learning, so that they are introduced to lives and possibilities outside their immediate environment. The positive meaning of being a child-centred early years environment is that you do not stop with children's current experience. You have a responsibility to show children something of the world beyond their own back door. You also have a responsibility for the future; many children will travel and leave their current local community.

Some people hold a restricted view that equal opportunities are only relevant for city areas, probably inner cities, because they have racial problems. The argument here is that if the local area has no black residents, then there are no problems and so no need for any equal opportunities initiatives. This mistaken outlook about metropolitan areas can be as misguided as the naïve views of some city dwellers about country life.

Mixed ethnic communities are not all divided by daily problems and ethnic strife, but disruption makes good newspaper headlines.

ISSUES IN A NON-DIVERSE AREA

Without an ethnically diverse local population, it is possible to feel that equal opportunities remain more theoretical than real. The advantage of a mixed local area is undoubtedly that there are real children and families who experience differences in dress, beliefs, diet and language. The challenge in a non-diverse area is to present materials to extend children's horizons, whilst showing that daily life is different not so far away within their own country, perhaps no more than an hour or so by car or train.

The details of equal opportunities should be adjusted for local issues, but any team needs to tackle what is appropriate for their area and what is an avoidance of the issues. Equal opportunities should extend beyond the current local population. For instance, if your local community were made up mainly of white English, nominally Christian families, and Muslim families who were mainly of African origin, it would be inappropriate to say, 'That's two religions and two sources of ethnic origin, so we don't need to think about what life is like in other parts of England or anywhere else around the world.'

The advantage of a diverse area is the greater likelihood of being able to consult many parents, to learn from them and involve them in your work. In an area with very little diversity, the parents from the very few minority ethnic groups may be called upon as the only example of a particular cultural tradition, language, or ethnic group. Some sensitivity is called for; think about how you might feel in their position. Parents may not want to be walking visual aids in your setting's project and, without some research work on your part, you may not be able to judge whether one parent is giving a rounded picture of a particular culture or faith.

A review of your play materials is appropriate because of your concern about what all children are learning about the world. You do not get black dolls for the pre-school because Yinka and his family have recently moved into the community. So, it is also inappropriate to ask Yinka's parents if they want black dolls or if they think you ought to get some different books. Families who are and feel very much in the minority locally are less likely to say 'yes' to such questions, especially if the accompanying message is that the setting's financial resources are being stretched just for them. Again, you would celebrate Chinese New Year as an opportunity for all the children to learn. It should never be the case of doing it because of Li-Fong and her family who run the local take-away.

There may be genuine practical problems of finding resources in an area with little ethnic diversity. Local book shops or toy suppliers may offer a range that assumes everyone is white, or that the few non-white families are exotic, temporary visitors. You may need to obtain materials through the many mail order book or play material suppliers (see page 193). But this is also true for many settings in diverse areas, where shops still do not reflect the full variety of families living locally.

ACTIVITY

Sometimes a team in a non-diverse area will say that equal opportunities on ethnic group and culture is nothing to do with them. Since the children do not apparently experience cultural variation, workers claim that it should not enter the curriculum. If such feelings are strong in some of your team, try the following exercise.

Find a map and draw a circle 20 miles in all directions around your setting. Now, imagine that you have to remove anything from your centre that children could neither see nor hear within that circle. The activity will be more effective if you physically make a pile of play materials. But, if you do not relish the tidying up, then make a list. For instance:

▶ Are you within 20 miles of the sea? If not, then out go any books, jigsaws or pictures about the seaside, sea fishing or seagoing boats. And perhaps the sand tray should be removed as well!
▶ What animals and birds can the children see in the local area? Remove any animals, domesticated or wild, that they will not encounter. So take away any books and pictures and any small-scale animals unless children can see the real thing locally. The same goes for flowers, trees and shrubs.
▶ Remove anything that relates to castles, forts or palaces, unless you have a real one nearby. The same goes for markets, circuses, fairs or anything else outdoors.
▶ Remove any books, pictures, construction material, play people or dressing-up clothes that do not reflect just what children can observe within the 20 mile boundary.
▶ And what if the children are not be allowed to draw anything they could not observe in their own everyday lives?

You will probably not get far into the activity before most people say that it is ridiculous to remove all these learning materials from children. Of course, it would be very foolish to organise a setting in this way. Children's learning is seriously restricted if the only permitted sources of play and ideas are those which can be personally experienced. So any group that has started by saying equal opportunities and culture is nothing to do with them needs to reflect on why they feel they can justify this view by reference to the limitations of their local area.

Children's language and behaviour

Please read this section together with the suggestions in the section on conversations with children (from page 21). All the issues discussed also apply to considerations of cultural and ethnic background.

QUESTIONS

Children are curious and often genuinely want to know the answer to questions like 'why is Clement black?' or 'is Satvinder a girl then, because he's got plaits?' Children may not always express their questions as courteously as they could, but part of your role is to help them to find more polite ways of asking questions. You may answer that Satvinder is definitely a boy, but he is a young Sikh boy and Sikh males do not cut their hair. Satvinder has his hair neatly wound onto his head until he is older when he will first have a small hair covering and then, as a young man, a turban.

OFFENSIVE REMARKS

Honest questions are not the same as rude remarks, but offensive comments and name calling are a fact of life for many children. Studies of primary school experiences, for instance by Cecile Wright, or Barry Troyna and Richard Hatcher (full references on page 121), have described the distress and daily problems for children when racist abuse is not effectively tackled by a school. Several useful points emerge from this research:

▶ Any setting should deal actively with overt racist remarks and incidents (see the suggestions on page 23).
▶ Workers in early years, playwork or school settings should never assume that arguments or even fights between children of visibly different ethnic groups are automatically racist. Good practice, as in any altercation between children, has to be that you ask and listen, but do not leap to conclusions about the rights and wrongs of the situation.
▶ Children sometimes put up with name calling or verbal bullying in order to be accepted by a group, or to avoid worse bullying. A child may then not appear to be hurt. Under these circumstances, probably

more likely in school than an early years setting, it would be wise to speak with the child in private, rather than speak up on his or her behalf. You might start by asking, 'How do you feel about Tracy and her friends calling you names?' and you could be honest with the child and explain, 'I'm not happy about it. I think it was very rude.'

▶ A firm approach to racist remarks or behaviour should be an integral part of any setting's behaviour policy, including the approach to bullying. Any setting has to balance up the adults' awareness of inequalities and discrimination within society, with a realisation that the children did not create this society.

▶ Young children are far less likely to support their peers if they experience a 'hierarchy of hurt' in practice – that hurtful remarks made to some children seem to matter more to the adults. A white child will be very hurt by a black peer who taunts, 'You're adopted. That means your mother didn't love you!' She should be supported in just the same way as the child who is on the receiving end of distressing racist remarks.

▶ It matters what children say but their attitudes are in the process of forming and you have a chance to influence them. It will not help to label a child as 'racist', any more than you should label them as 'aggressive', 'lazy' or 'spiteful'. Negative labels do not help a child to find another way of reacting. Affirm the child as a person; you are reacting to the unacceptable words, not to them as an individual.

FOCUS ON CHILDREN'S BEHAVIOUR

Good practice is to listen to children in general and to what they want to say about an incident. You may rightly say that you do not want *any* of these racist words used, but you will get further if you understand the children's situation, including who did what, to whom and when.

Some children use racist abuse with full understanding and the intention of hurting. But some children, especially younger ones, may use a term without understanding what they are saying. Children also sometimes say that offensive words just pop out, without definite intention, at times of stress, like forbidden swear words. They may also be used in retaliation to a previous insult, for instance a white girl shouts 'coon' at a black peer who has just called her a 'lezzie'.

In any emotionally charged situation, children will take more notice of adults who are clearly listening to what has happened and are not applying rigid rules or unfairly taking one child's side over that of another. Adults also need to be clear with children, and often for themselves, about what behaviour is expected of all the children. For instance, it certainly is not the case that everyone has to be nice to Aaron because he is Jewish. On the other hand, nobody should be offensive to Aaron just because he and his family are Jewish. If Aaron is annoying and disrupts a game, then this situation needs to be resolved, but not through anti-semitic abuse.

ADULT EXPECTATIONS OF CHILDREN

Children's behaviour is shaped, at least to some extent, by how adults react. Adults are, in their turn, affected by their expectations, because of the social or cultural group to which children belong. In Chapter 2 (see page 43) there is a description of how gender stereotypes can shape adults' reactions to boys and girls, leading to positive or negative interpretations. Some workers have especially poor expectations of African-Caribbean boys' behaviour. Cecile Wright noted that African-Caribbean boys were amongst the most criticised and reprimanded in the mixed classrooms which she observed. The boys were told off for the kind of behaviour that was often ignored for white children. The black boys were more prominent in school discipline procedures, such as being sent out of the classroom, and exclusions. Wright's observations are supported by national exclusion statistics. Boys feature more than girls overall, but African-Caribbean boys are being excluded at about six times the national average for any group of pupils. These problems seem to have their roots in the boys' early school and pre-school experience. So, early years workers, playworkers and staff of reception classes can make a difference. Several issues seem to be involved:

▶ Some workers have stereotypical beliefs about African-Caribbean families, for instance that all parents use harsh, physical discipline and so the boys will be very energetic or disruptive away from home. This attitude can lead workers to treat the boys differently from other children, allowing them to restrict their play experience to lively, mainly outdoors play.

▶ All cultures have some variety in use of spoken language and body language. Some communication styles of African-Caribbean families are more direct and boys especially may be seen by workers as cheeky or argumentative. The usual dangers of labelling a child can follow and boys start a career as a 'troublemaker'.

▶ Unless a setting has a clear policy setting out a positive approach to children's behaviour, negative judgements may be shared amongst a staff team, so that children have fewer and fewer options. Adults become more fearful of losing a power struggle with the boys, than of tackling behaviour with appropriate discipline.

▶ Boys need early years experience that develops positive attitudes towards learning (see the discussion on page 62). African-Caribbean boys may especially need appropriate male role models, ideally black male workers, to counteract many of the messages within society that lead them away from self esteem in a learning environment such as a school.

FOR EXAMPLE:

Daniel is the leader of Falcon Square After School Club. The club is in an ethnically mixed city area and picks up children from several local primary schools. The play team takes a firm anti-racist approach and has been pleased to see children forming friendships across the ethnic and religious diversity within the local community. In a recent team meeting, Daniel and his colleagues have become more aware of the pressures on the children from their families. Two particular instances have arisen lately through children's conversations:

▶ Lucy has developed a close friendship with Maria. They spend a great deal of time together at the club and during the school day. It has emerged that several times Lucy has been invited to play at Maria's house and wants to go, but Lucy's parents find every excuse to refuse the invitations. There seems to be no other reason except that Maria is black. Lucy's (white) parents have been heard making racist remarks, when they think they are out of earshot of the staff.

▶ Shamima is a popular girl at the club. She gets on well with many of the other children and is often asked to birthday parties or to come for tea. The staff have recently overheard a conversation between parents: 'There's no point in asking Shamima to birthday parties. She never comes and her parents don't even have the courtesy to answer invitations.' Daniel has explored what appears to be happening and finds that Shamima's parents only ever accept invitations from other Muslim households.

The club team are divided about whether these two examples are much the same. Some workers feel that both Lucy's and Shamima's parents are being equally rejecting and that the team should at least consider saying something. Other workers feel that the religious beliefs of Shamima's parents make their behaviour more acceptable, although perhaps they should recognise that some children's feelings are hurt. The whole team is wrestling with how they should draw the boundary between what happens in the club and parents' decisions about their private, family life.

QUESTIONS

1 What are the main issues raised here? The workers in the club are taking different perspectives – what are these?
2 Is this a situation in which the workers have a positive role to play and, if so, what might that be? What might you do in this situation?
3 How might the children feel – all the children involved in the current situation?

Use of resources

Play and learning resources matter in any early years, school or playwork setting. But, of course, excellent books or a well-stocked music cupboard will not create good practice on their own. A great deal depends on how workers introduce and use resources.

▶ Your aim is to reflect the cultural traditions represented in your current group, the local community and other areas in easy travelling distance from where you are based.
▶ Your equally important aim is to extend the horizons of the children. So you will need to make some choices, but will not be restricted to cultural traditions represented locally.
▶ All traditions should be approached with respect and you should avoid any implication that the main traditions within the current group are more normal than the other exotic or odd traditions that you explore briefly. This approach is sometimes called a **tourist curriculum** because the impression given is that the activities are not related to real life.
▶ Whatever the composition of your group, workers are responsible for encouraging attitudes of respect as well as interest. For instance, it would be no more acceptable for a mainly African-Caribbean group of children to ridicule Japanese clothes, religious festivals or food, than it would be to allow such behaviour from a mainly white group of children.

Any staff team needs to be clear about the reasons for looking carefully at their resources. If you are clear, you will be better able to explain to parents who are confused about your motives. There have been some misleading media reports about introducing a range of cultural traditions. A frequent misunderstanding is that respect for one culture must reduce the level of respect for what has been regarded as the mainstream tradition. Efforts to extend experience of food and ways of eating have led to foolish headlines about groups supposedly removing all the cutlery from nurseries or claiming that eating 'curry' would stop little children being racist.

EQUAL OPPORTUNITIES ARE RELEVANT TO EVERYONE

You need to seek a positive identity for all the children. Much of this chapter raises awareness that, because of the racist attitudes common in society, children from minority ethnic groups may develop low self-esteem. However, an enthusiastic use of resources from a wide range of different cultural traditions can leave white children feeling that all the interesting material comes from cultures other than their own. You want all the children to develop a positive sense of history and culture for all the groups to which they and their family belong.

Studies of white children in socially deprived areas have highlighted that they may have no obvious sources of positive identity unless they are disdainful and rejecting of black groups. An approach that stresses other cultures may not only increase feelings of 'them and us', but fail to help white children to explore their own sources of personal, family and cultural identity in a way that could counteract prejudiced feelings of superiority. Any programme to help children of ethnic minorities find positive identities and explore their history needs to be grounded in an overview of how all the children are likely to gain a sense of pride in their origins.

PARTNERSHIP WITH PARENTS

You will have experience and knowledge within your staff team, but good working relationships with parents will open more possibilities. Parents can be a good source of ideas, of knowledge and of the explanations often necessary when you do not have first-hand experience of a culture. Some parents may be pleased to spend some time in the setting and support singing, cooking or storytelling activities. Partnership will work well if you bear the following in mind:

▶ Parents should be able to choose the extent to which they are involved. Some mothers or fathers will have more time, interest or the confidence to become involved with a project.

▶ Avoid a restricted view that workers only ask Winston's mother about Caribbean cookery, Liam's family about anything Irish and Ujala's family about Indian dancing. All these parents may be pleased to share their experience, but they will also have a range of other talents and skills.

▶ Note also that adults are not necessarily experts on their own cultural traditions. Try asking a random group of white English parents about the origins of May Day celebrations, how to do morris dancing or make a traditional Lancashire hotpot; many will have very little idea.

It will also be important that you explore traditions that are not represented in the families who attend your setting. Even in a diverse local community, there will be some traditions with which nobody is familiar. It could be a positive experience for your team and the children to approach a topic on which nobody has direct experience. There is much to learn for everyone in doing your own research.

Personal histories

Any family that has moved country or continent within recent generations could be described as having a country of origin as well as their current roots. Some families whose origins are minority ethnic are of recent arrival in Britain, but some have lived here for many years, in some cases for generations. I recall a student welcoming party some years ago in which the only black female student was being asked in measured tones by a well-meaning member of staff, 'How do you like the university so far?' and, 'Have you travelled far to study here?' The reply in a clear Welsh accent was, 'It's fine' and, 'A fair way. I'm from Cardiff.' The follow-up question of, 'But where did you come from originally?' was met with, 'Still Cardiff.'

There will always be variety in how families will see themselves and workers need to be aware of their own unchecked assumptions. Some families retain strong cultural and religious traditions and live in communities where the key values are shared. Some will retain such links and also feel a strong allegiance to Britain. Children raised in Britain are likely to feel like black British or Asian British. It is important, and courteous, that you do not make assumptions about children's allegiances. For instance, you should ask a general question of a mixed group such as, 'Has anyone any connections with India?' rather than homing in on one child with, 'India's your country, isn't it, Rajiv?'

Increasingly children and young people want to carve out an identity that feels right to them and is an accurate reflection of all their sources of identity. Studies of children of mixed parentage in Britain and the United States are beginning to show their irritation with adults, who are part of a different generation, telling them that they must view their identity in a particular way: for instance, that children with one black and one white parent should see themselves as black. Children and young people often want to develop an identity that reflects all their allegiances and heritage.

Older children can explore a wide range of project work

ACTIVITY

Part of all children's personal identity is their family history. You could develop a project on family time lines. Whatever the extent of ethnic group diversity in your local community, you will be able to explore whether local families have moved around the country, or between countries. Several considerations will help you to make this project a positive experience:

▶ Talk with parents about the plans for the project and reassure them, if necessary, that you are not delving into their family history out of nosiness.

▶ Make sure that each family's time line is treated with equal interest and respect. Families who have lived in the area for generations are as interesting as those who have family origins in other countries.

▶ The families with strong local roots may take you towards an exploration of history. For instance, you might want to find out what was happening at the same time as Sara's great-grandparents were running the farm. You might discover that Hamish's family lived in the area when the shipbuilding yards were still open.

▶ Families who have moved country recently, or in past generations, may be a direct way to make sense of geography for children, as may the experience of traveller families (see page 110).

▶ Be aware and sensitive about refugee families whose moves will not
   have been a matter of choice, but forced by war and other political
   disruptions (see page 113).

Creative play activities

The very wide range of arts and crafts, drawing from many cultural traditions,
can be a rich source of activities for children, of displays and of visits to
suitable local exhibitions. As with any other type of resource it would not, of
course, be sensible to overwhelm young children with many different kinds
of work in quick succession. Any early years or playwork setting can steadily
gather a file of ideas, and your local library may be a valuable source of craft
books with clear illustrations and advice on basic technique. Some crafts will
be technically too difficult for young children, or involve unrealistic levels of
one-to-one supervision. But the more challenging crafts might be a source of
striking displays of pictures or ready-made items.

PRINTING AND DYEING

Batik is an Indonesian word that describes a form of printing on material
when hot wax is used to resist a dye. A similar technique is used in parts of
India and Africa to produce striking bolts of cloth which are wrapped
around women, or men, to create clothing and head coverings. Batik is not
a suitable technique for use in nursery or even primary school but children
can be interested in how the cloth is produced. The material makes a very
effective display along with photographs of clothing.

Basic printing techniques on paper, card or cloth can be explored with thick
paint and different shapes, which could include a wide range of fruit and
vegetables (like potato printing). Wax crayon can be used on paper as a
resist, and paint applied on top. Tie dyeing is a potentially simpler technique
which also has its origins in Indian craft techniques.

USE OF MATERIAL

Traditions of patchwork and of plaiting used material often developed in
communities where thrift was crucial. The current generation of children
can be interested in such traditions for their environmental friendliness as
well as the richness of texture, shape and colour that is possible with even
the simpler designs.

The ancient Egyptians and Peruvians used fabric created from plaited strips
of used material. The white European settlers on the east coast of the United

States used the method in order to recycle worn-out clothes and plaiting oval and circular rugs is a traditional English country craft.

Patchwork has a rich artistic tradition but, once again, has its roots in economy, for some communities could afford to waste nothing. There are many books on patchwork – both traditional English designs and the slightly different approach of white European settlers in the United States. Some religious communities, for instance the Amish in Pennsylvania, would not use patterned fabric, yet created stunning designs with use of colour and quilting techniques. Patchwork and appliqué designs are also traditional in parts of India and the Far East, including Indonesia.

ACTIVITY

Buy or borrow from the library a few books on patchwork. Choose a few designs and use these to explore with the children:

▶ The different basic shapes used in the design and how the individual shapes make an overall pattern.
▶ How colour (light, dark and patterned) can change the nature of a design, making first one part and then another come to the fore.
▶ If you work with older children, they may be ready to manage some basic sewing. Young children will enjoy working with material, or stiff paper, shapes (some of which they can have cut themselves), moving the parts around until the design is complete and then sticking them down onto backing fabric or card.
▶ Talk with parents. You may find that some of them own or actually make patchwork and would be happy to contribute to a display.
▶ This creative project could also be linked into a recycling theme.

Knitting and Crochet

Young children will find the techniques of knitting too difficult, but could be involved in a project about use of colour and the different styles of knitting. Traditional British designs, for instance, the Aran jumper or dark blue Jersey style were developed as working clothes, to keep out the cold and damp of working on the land or at sea.

Weaving, Threading and Embroidery

Jewellery is part of many cultural traditions in dress, although styles vary. Children could explore use of jewellery as everyday decoration as well as accessories for special occasions – for men as well as for women in some cultures. Even young children can make simple jewellery by bead threading. A combination of beadwork, embroidery and use of reflective materials such as small mirrors can be seen in different styles of dress, including some Asian traditions. Bead threading is a traditional craft of Africa, of North American Indians and also in South America.

Weaving is an important craft in many countries around the world. Cloth is woven and, with different techniques, rugs and carpets are produced. Children can learn simple weaving techniques on a card or small wooden loom.

Star weaving is a craft that uses a simple technique of winding wool or other thread around two crossed sticks to produce star designs that vary in colour, texture and size. The star weavings are most common in Latin America, where they are known in Spanish as *Ojos de Dios* – God's Eyes. The completed weavings are symbolic of a request that the eye of God (or of gods) should watch over someone, often a child. Similar weavings are also found in parts of Africa and the Far East.

PAINTING AND DRAWING

Different styles of drawing and painting reflect varied cultural traditions and children can appreciate looking at pictures or exhibitions at local galleries as much as working on their own designs.

Different European painting traditions, from across the centuries, can open children's eyes to the many different ways to paint, draw and sketch. The bold lines of some African traditions of painting or the Australian Aborigines' pictures can show children another style. Such designs contrast with the intricate patterns of Celtic knotwork or the flowers and complex geometric shapes of Muslim art. Traditional shapes such as the circles and spirals of Celtic art would be difficult for children to draw from scratch, but are ideal for the fine coordinations learned through tracing some of the patterns or colouring the shapes.

SELF PORTRAITS

Children also want to draw themselves and their friends. Any setting needs a supply of skin colour toned paints and crayons so that children can achieve subtle differences in skin colour.

COLLAGE

This word comes from the French *papier collé* and means literally the art of sticking anything onto a background in order to make a picture. This craft, traditional to England as well as other countries, is appropriate for even young children, since the technique can be kept very simple. A wide range of materials can be stuck onto a firm background: fabric, coloured and textured paper, lace, dried flowers and the modern material of dried pasta. Small cut-out pictures, for instance, of flowers can be built up on a base, like a tray or a box, and then varnished in the Victorian English tradition of decoupage (from the French, *découpage*).

Traditional games for children

Some schools and early years settings have worked to reintroduce a range of traditional games to children in the garden or the playground. With adults' increasing concern about children's safety outside the home, it seems that children are losing the opportunity to pass on games from one generation to another. Early years and playworkers can use this opportunity to ensure that games come from a range of cultural traditions. Organisations such as UNICEF or Oxfam (see addresses on page 193) often have booklets in their catalogues about games from around the world.

Two books are sources of some ideas to consider:
Gyles Brandreth (1992) *Children's Games* (Chancellor Press)
Lorriane Barbarash (1997) *Multicultural Games* (Human Kinetics)

ACTIVITY

Compare memories with colleagues, or fellow students, about the games that you played as a child with other children.

▶ What materials did you use, if any?
▶ What were the rules and were there any songs or sayings (for instance skipping chants) that accompanied the games?
▶ Consider the games that you have collected and decide which could be suitable for your current group of children. Think about the content of the game and the words in any chants.

Displays and illustrations

As well as the displays that you create from children's drawings or craft work, you will also use a range of different illustrations around your setting: posters, postcards, magazine pictures and photo montage. Any images need to be balanced so that all the children can see themselves in the visual material, alongside some positive images of children and families who may not be represented locally. Balance in illustrations is just as important in the baby room, if you take very young children in your setting. Babies and toddlers are looking around them and noticing. Also their parents will be coming every day and they should be able to see themselves in the posters and notice boards around your setting.

A QUESTION OF BALANCE

The key issue is the balance of images that you portray and an awareness of what else children are likely to see, in your setting or elsewhere.

▶ Charity catalogues can be a useful source of materials to extend the cultural traditions represented in your setting. A number of the organisations listed on page 193 produce sets of photographs and posters. Some sell yearly diaries that include striking pictures of children and their families from around the world.

▶ But you have to be cautious about using charity posters whose aim is fundraising. You would not, after all, resource a project on domestic animals only from the fundraising material of the RSPCA.

▶ Travel brochures can be a good source of pictures of many different countries, but they need to be balanced with more everyday images of families shopping, at mealtimes or children at school. Children need to understand other countries and cultures through shared experiences as much as the possible differences.

▶ The weekend colour magazines can be a good source of pictures to be cut out and made into a display. The National Geographic Magazine has stunning photographs and back copies often end up in second-hand bookshops.

TO THINK ABOUT

If white children only, or mainly, see African or Indian children as part of appeals for charity aid, then it is highly likely that they will develop an image of all black families as poverty-stricken and in need of help. When resources are unbalanced, black children will also be puzzled or uneasy about images that have nothing to do with their own lives.

White children's self-image is unlikely to be affected by sad white faces, perhaps on posters for the NSPCC. White children have many other images from which to build a sense of self. In a similar way, black British children are very unlikely to think, from seeing charity posters for homeless families or the work of the Salvation Army, that all white children are sad and badly treated – because there are so many alternative images.

Play materials

DOLLS, PLAY PEOPLE AND PUPPETS

Dolls are important because they represent people (babies, children and adults) and children use them in a broad range of play. A setting needs a range of dolls and play people of the two sexes, different ages and ethnic backgrounds. Dolls are often not accurate portrayals of babies or children; there is an element of simplification or even caricature in the features or the body's proportions. When children have plenty of positive images from which to feed their sense of personal identity, then mild caricatures matter less, because they fade into the background of more accurate and positive images. If children have few positive images, than a great deal will depend on those few images that they can see of themselves in the dolls, or any other play resources.

It is possible now, unlike a couple of decades ago, to buy proper black dolls with different features and hair from the white ones, and not just white dolls with European features which have been produced with dark skin. Also, it is preferably that dolls should be dark in their whole body and not just the faces – whether these are firm or rag dolls. Children often love caring for dolls' hair and African or Caribbean dolls with proper hair can give children the chance to braid their hair. Suppliers also produce a whole range of families for dolls' houses.

TO THINK ABOUT

Discussion about dolls for young children often leads to a conversation, or argument, about golliwogs. Some white adults have had a cherished golliwog in their own childhood and older adults may have collected the badges when Robertsons gave paper cutouts and metal badges. This situation is one which requires sceptical white adults to make the effort to look through the eyes of black children and really think about how they would feel if a caricature were all that was available to support their own self-image.

If you are a white reader, imagine that almost all the characters in the books of your childhood were black. In your nursery or school there was a much-loved book that had a white character, Pinochio. This little boy was also produced as a doll and was the only doll in nursery or toy shops that had a white face. The other children called you and the few other white boys and girls 'Noky' and made offensive remarks about the length of your nose and that it grew because you told lies. The black adults knew you were upset but would not take your distress seriously. Your parents were told, 'Noky dolls are part of everyone's childhood. It's nothing personal, it's just a doll. Anyway children don't notice things like that.'

> ▶ Try hard to put yourself into this imagined situation. How would you have felt as a child?
> ▶ How might you feel as an adult looking back, especially one who is now being told that you're making a fuss about nothing?

JIGSAWS

Much the same issues arise with jigsaws as with any illustrated play materials. Make sure that you have a full range of everyday scenes and of people, as well as the illustrations that may be more impressionistic. It is now possible to buy jigsaws that show children and families from a range of different ethnic backgrounds.

THE HOME CORNER

Children will use the home corner to explore and play out everyday events and relationships. It is not the only focus of their pretend play, but can be a rich source of ideas and of props. It is possible to obtain child-sized cooking equipment and different utensils that reflect different styles of cooking and eating. As well as pots and pans, you can have bowls, woks, ladles, large chopsticks or a steaming basket.

This area of play and learning is one in which adults have to be wary of their own assumptions. For instance, English kitchens frequently have a kettle but in many other European countries a kettle is not a usual item of equipment; you boil water in a small saucepan. Asian families usually make tea in a saucepan and not a tea pot. In various parts of the Mediterranean or Africa proper coffee is made in a small heat-proof container and not with instant powder. If you are unfamiliar with some cooking implements, then you may need to check how they are used.

DRESSING-UP CLOTHES

Children, boys and girls, like to dress up because they are trying out how to be adults. A range of clothes will help them to explore relationships, familiar or unfamiliar, and children need to see clothing that is commonplace to them as well as styles that are less well known. A full range includes everyday clothing as well as special occasion clothes.

Depending on your experience, you may need to check whether a set of clothes are special or ordinary wear in a given culture. For instance, in Britain men wear top hats and tails for formal occasions. Japanese women do not wear kimonos as everyday wear on the streets of Tokyo, but they are more common for special occasions such as weddings. However, Welsh traditional women's dress, with the shawl, long skirt and large dark hat is only likely to be worn at cultural events or where people are dressing up for historical reasons.

A good dressing-up clothes rail has a range of skirts, tops and tunics, trousers, wraps, hats and other head coverings. If your setting is used by families of a varied ethnic background then many of your clothes may be contributions from parents. You may need to supplement these with purchases from some of the suppliers listed on page 193. As well as different kinds of European style dress, you can have shalwar kameez (the tunic and full trousers worn by some Asian girls and women). Lengths of uncut fabric can be draped around children to make an Indian-style sari or the wrap around clothing styles of men and women in parts of Africa and the Far East.

Headgear can include hats and flat caps, head scarves, skull caps and turbans (worn not only by Sikh men but also by both men and women of some North African ethnic groups).

Children may need some further background to make sense of what you are providing, especially if the clothes are not seen on your local streets. Displays, books and photographs can supplement children's everyday experience to show that ordinary people, adults and children, wear this style of clothing in other parts of Britain as well as other countries. Children, and your own team, need to extend their understanding of different kinds of dress, especially when unfamiliar forms are initially confusing. For instance, Scots men who wear a kilt are not dressing up as women any more than an Indian man in a dhoti or a Nigerian in a wrappa.

Careful intervention will be necessary if children use the clothes as funny disguises, since their play could then reinforce stereotypes about ethnic groups that are, or are not, represented in the setting. Dressing up should be enjoyable, but not a vehicle for making fun of other people. You should discourage any joke Indian accents when children put on a sari, as much as any mock Scots ones if they experiment with kilts.

BOOKS

The key issues in looking at your book collection are very similar to those expressed on page 61 about boys and girls and on page 177 about disabled children:

▶ Can children in your group see themselves in the books on your shelves, that you read to the children and that you borrow from your local library?

▶ Are there children of visibly different ethnic groups, children and adults of mixed parentage, traveller as well as settled families?

▶ Can children, even in a setting with very little apparent ethnic diversity, see variety in the fiction and non-fiction books that you share with them? Are your books, along with all the other play materials, extending children's understanding of the world beyond their own doorstep?

▶ How do children of different ethnic groups appear in the books? Are they heroes and heroines as well as followers? Are they sometimes simply getting on with their lives, or is their ethnic group and skin colour often made into a problem? Do books give the false impression that minority ethnic families only live in inner city areas?

Books can be a good source of information and interest

Any setting needs a full collection of modern fiction for children, but they also enjoy traditional folk tales and myths and legends. These books can be drawn from a range of cultural or religious traditions. Some books offer a world-wide selection while others focus on African, Asian, Celtic or American Indian traditions. Always read any folk tales or legends to yourself before reading them aloud to children. Some are fairly bloodthirsty or have a strong sexual theme. You may want to think twice about some of the stories with younger groups.

Storytelling can be an enjoyable supplement to reading from books. You may be fortunate to have someone local who is a skilled storyteller, and some early years and playworkers become good storytellers with books that they have learned by heart. As with the books in your setting, aim for a range of traditions represented by the stories. If your local resources are limited, then consider extending them with audio tapes or recording some of the excellent children's television programmes that feature storytelling.

Some books about 'children from other lands' can be very informative, but make sure that you are not giving children, especially in a mainly white area, the inaccurate idea that all black people live abroad. You also need books that feature children and their families in different towns, cities and the countryside of Britain. Look carefully at any books on children around the world to ensure that they do not give an unbalanced image, perhaps that African children only live in rural areas, when the truth is that many live in towns and cities.

Be ready to prune books if your setting takes over a motley collection or you are given boxes of books. You are not acting unreasonably as a censor. Responsible early years and playworkers should always make a considered decision about books for content and presentation. You never buy them by the yard or because the colour of the covers matches the decor of your setting.

MUSIC, SONGS AND DANCE

Children enjoy songs and rhymes, with or without hand movements. Awareness of sound and sound patterns is helped by participation in a group or performance when an individual child enjoys standing up to deliver a chosen song or rhyme. You can ensure that the children's repertoire includes songs from different cultural traditions and you may be fortunate in having parents who could sing for children in languages other than English. Audio tapes are also available to supplement live singing sessions. Tapes are often sold with written song books and short explanatory leaflets giving the background to the songs.

Most musical traditions have at least some simple instruments that can be used by young children. You can choose from a wide range of small drums, single stringed instruments, flutes and simple whistles, xylophones, many different kinds of shakers, bells that may be shaken, small sets of bells (like gungroos) that are worn on the wrist or ankles and make music as children dance, cymbals and tambourines.

Musical activities need to be presented positively:

▶ Children can enjoy themselves, practise fine physical coordinations and learn to play their instruments in particular rhythms, for instance, light Caribbean calypso rhythms or the steady thump of an English marching band.

▶ It is important that all the instruments are treated with equal interest and respect and that the same applies when you listen to different kinds of music with the children on tape or CD.

▶ Use the correct name for any instrument and talk a little with children about each instrument, even those that you expect will be familiar to them. Some musical instruments will be unfamiliar to you, but you will usually find information either in the catalogue or in leaflets sent with instruments.

▶ Never refer to 'ethnic instruments' as this term creates a negative division between 'our music' or even 'proper music' in contrast with everything else. Caribbean steel pans are no more an 'ethnic instrument' than the violin, which has a central place in English country dancing and Irish Celtic music, although in this context it will probably be known as a fiddle.

When you listen to music, there may be a slight delay as children and adults adjust to unfamiliar musical forms. Some instruments, like bagpipes, can make an unsettling sound until the musician moves into the tune. Children do not have to like all forms of music, although they are very likely to be keen on some of the styles which you introduce to them. Much like encouraging children to try different kinds of food, you should establish a ground rule that, after proper listening, anyone can say they do not particularly like the music, but not that it is 'stupid', 'rubbish' or 'not real music'.

If you are lucky, you may be able to invite a local musical or dance group into your setting, or take the children to a display. Otherwise, you can be creative and use video and tapes of music, dance and song from a range of cultural traditions.

FOOD AND DRINK

Exploration of different traditions in food and drink offers several strands for children's learning:

▶ Children can be involved in buying a range of ingredients, such as fruit and vegetables, spices and seasonings, and basics like eggs or flour. Some readers may be lucky and work near a market, which is an excellent way for children to see how food starts, rather than only experiencing the finished meal. The main supermarket chains now carry a much wider choice of food than used to be the case and from many different culinary traditions.

▶ Depending on the age of the children and the facilities in your setting, you may be able to explore some real cooking activities. If you cannot allow children into the kitchen you may be able to prepare food together and then hand it over to the cook.

▶ The range of food offered to the children in a full-day or even a sessional early years setting can reflect more than one cultural tradition and should certainly include the traditions of the children who attend.

▶ Even if you work in a setting without a kitchen or you do not give children a full meal, you can still explore different kinds of food and drink. Look creatively at the possibilities for snack time or for a non-cooked tea that is given to children. You could try, perhaps after a shopping trip with the children, different kinds of bread – leavened and unleavened – some fruit or vegetables that are unfamiliar to some children and cakes or biscuits from different cultural traditions.

Within any cultural tradition there are variations from area to area. For instance, every Indian family certainly does not eat spicy food. Southern Indian food is generally more highly spiced than Northern. Some Indians are vegetarians, whereas others eat meat and poultry. In the same way, all English families do not sit down every Sunday to roast beef and Yorkshire pudding. So, make sure you avoid giving children the impression that everyone from a given group eats particular food.

If you can organise some simple cooking or food preparation with the children, then bear in mind that key techniques can then be used to make different kinds of food. For instance, once children learn to make a basic bread dough, the group can produce different shapes of English bread or buns. Slight variations in the basic recipe can produce Irish soda bread or unleavened kinds of bread like chapatis and puris, Jewish matzo bread and Mexican tortillas. Breads like puris that have to be fried could be handed over to the nursery or school cook for finishing. A basic batter mixture can, with slight variations, lead to English-style pancakes, thin French crêpes, the thicker Scotch pancakes or tempura (Japanese fritters).

Any cooking activities or variation in nursery lunches and snacks should, of course, respect any dietary needs in the group, whether these are food allergies or religious and cultural traditions about what is, or is not, eaten by individual families (see page 134). With care, you can widen children's perspective on food and also explore different ways of eating. It is valuable for all children to be able to use cutlery in the English way, since this skill will give them flexibility in their adult life. However, you can introduce different ways of eating to the group as you explore a range of foods. Some cultural traditions use cutlery, while others have different traditions for eating meals and snacks:

▶ Even European-style knives and forks are not used in the same way everywhere. Americans, for instance, tend to cut up the meal, transfer the fork to the right hand and then fork the prepared food into their mouths.

▶ In China, Japan and other parts of the Far East chopsticks are the common utensils for eating and larger versions are used in cooking. If you are going to let the children try using chopsticks, then make sure you have learned how to handle them, if you are unfamiliar. Try to recall how long young children take to learn to manipulate a knife and fork. An alternative, when children will not spend a long time learning, is to make a simpler children's utensil with two shorter chopsticks, about 20 cm long. Place a 2 cm length of stick or card between the two sticks about 2–3 cm from the top and bind with an elastic band.

▶ Some Asian and African traditions involve eating with the fingers and perhaps using the different kinds of bread to guide some of the food. Using bread is also an English tradition, although more to finish off a meal especially one with sauce or gravy.

TO THINK ABOUT

English adults in childhood were often given a hard time about eating with their fingers, as people think it is dirty. So they unthinkingly repeat these words in an early years or school setting. In fact clean fingers can be far more hygienic than cutlery, especially poorly cleaned knives or forks.

Children will not like all the meals or foods that they try and a fair ground rule is that children can say they are not keen, but nobody is rude about the food, saying 'yuk, disgusting!' or similar remarks. Such ground rules apply to everyone. It is just as unreasonable for a child of African-Caribbean origin to reject out of hand 'that horrid Paki food' as a white child to say that 'all Chinese food is rubbish'.

FESTIVALS AND CELEBRATIONS

Some festivals are mainly religious but some, although they may have a religious origin, have become more secular celebrations. Early years, school and playwork settings have to make some choices, since everyone will be overwhelmed if different festivals follow hard on each other's heels. So consider a range of possibilities and do not assume that children necessarily know much about their own cultural traditions. You will find many ideas in Chapter 4 (page 139).

Personal issues for children and families

Names

For everyone, a name is part of your personal identity. It can feel anything from mildly discourteous to downright offensive if people do not try to say your name properly, or persist in versions that you do not want to be called. Children also deserve this attention and effort.

PRONUNCIATION AND SPELLING

Many of the practical issues that arise over names from a range of different cultural traditions are covered by general good practice. However, these issues may not be highlighted until you encounter names that are unfamiliar to you.

▶ It is good practice to ensure that you spell and say correctly the names of all the children and their parents. The guideline of 'if in doubt, ask' sums up courteous behaviour that applies in your relations with any family. If a name is unfamiliar to you, and initially you find it hard to say, then make yourself a reminder note on how to pronounce the child's name correctly. The children themselves may be happy to help you practise.

▶ Ensure that you write down the names of both parents, if there are two in the family. British families do not necessarily all share the same surname and some cultural traditions do not have a surname.

▶ Follow the child's and parents' wishes over how a child is known, if this name is not his/her full first name. Some children prefer to be called by a shortened version of their name or have more than one personal name and are not known by the first one.

▶ Certainly, workers should never shorten or change a child's name (or a colleague's for that matter) to avoid the small amount of effort needed to learn the proper name.

▶ Be sensitive in your first conversations with a family. If a child, or their parents, have previously experienced discourtesy about how to say or spell their name, they may agree to a simplification for an easy life. Their agreement does not mean that they genuinely wish for a name change.

▶ You can acknowledge that a name is unfamiliar to you with comments like, 'Can I make sure that I am saying your daughter's name correctly?' Avoid any suggestion that a name is odd and, certainly, most names are not difficult; you only find them hard to say because of unfamiliarity.

Young children sometimes struggle with some patterns of sound. If your name is a challenge for some children to say, then it is your choice to simplify it. All languages do not include the same range of sounds and some sounds can be hard to pronounce, although first language speakers will not see the potential difficulty.

FOR EXAMPLE:

My names probably look easy to readers whose first language is English. But my first name, Jennie, is hard to say for anyone whose first language does not include a hard 'j' sound, for instance, French. My surname, Lindon, is virtually impossible for English-speaking Japanese, because the 'l' sound is non-existent in Japanese, and tends to be replaced with an 'r'. I also frequently experience misspellings of both my names by English first-language writers because of the presumption that they are easy, so I am not asked how I spell them!

CULTURAL TRADITIONS IN NAMING SYSTEMS

In Britain the most familiar naming system has been that of one or more personal names followed by a family surname. The cultural tradition of calling the first names 'Christian names' arises because Christianity has been the world faith that most shaped British society. The religious tradition of christening babies as symbolic of their entering the church community established the idea of a 'Christian name'. (Not all Christian groups agree with christening babies; some baptise adults at an age when they are judged

Careful records become especially important with a culturally diverse local population

to be able to make their own decision to commit to the faith.) In a diverse society, with many faiths and many families who do not follow a given religious faith at all, the phrase 'Christian name' is no longer appropriate. 'First' or 'personal names' are a more accurate description.

You will also find different systems of surnames within white European culture. Traditionally in Britain, married women have taken their husband's surname, but several mainland European countries have a tradition of making a double-barrelled family name with both the surnames. In some countries women do not change their surname on marriage and children may also take her surname. British children have traditionally taken their father's surname, but not all families follow this pattern. Where children are part of stepfamilies, there may be more than one surname in the family. The guideline of 'don't assume, ask' is the best and simple approach. Again, it would be inappropriate and discourteous for early years workers to imply that the family names were confusing or some kind of problem.

The European system of naming is far from universal. If you work in a diverse area, you need to be aware of different cultural and religious traditions. Not everyone, by any means, places the personal name first of all. So you need to check with parents the name by which you should address a child, sometimes described as the 'calling name'. In many cultures there are some names which can be given either to boys or girls. The sex of babies or very young children is not always obvious. So, if you are in any doubt, then you do need to ask politely. Most cultural traditions give names, in addition to a personal name, but many do not include the idea that all members of a family will share the same name – the European surname. You should follow the parents' choice. Some examples of the variation in use of names follow:

▶ Chinese tradition follows a system that the family name (shared by all family members) comes first, then a generation name may follow (which places the person within the family) and then a personal name. So, if Shek Gai Wai is about to join your setting, you need to note that Shek is her family name, Gai indicates that she is a child in the family and Wai is her personal name. Vietnamese families follow a similar pattern.

▶ Hindu families place the personal name first, followed by another name such as bhai (brother) or devi (goddess). When children have a name that could be given to a boy or a girl, the second name will specify their sex. For instance Anu Kumar (prince) is a boy, whereas Anu Kumari (princess) is a girl. The last name for Hindu families is a shared family name that indicates the family's traditional status and occupation. This system led to many people having the same last name and Hindu practice is to record the father's or husband's name for extra identification. So, Anu Kumar might have the last name, Sharma, and Anu Kumari may take her father's name, Patel.

▶ Sikh tradition broke with Hinduism (see page 131) and with the last names that reflected the caste system. Devout Sikh families will still not use a last name, although many Sikhs in Britain do use a surname to make life more straightforward. So, children will have a personal name, followed by 'Kaur' (meaning princess) for a girl and 'Singh' (meaning lion) for a boy. So Paramjit Kaur may also have a last name, by which the family may all be known. If there is no last name, then her father should be called Mr Singh and her mother Mrs Kaur. If you are uncertain, then ask politely about any shared family name.

▶ Muslim boys are often given a personal and a religious name (Mohammed, Syed, Ali and other names of Allah). The religious name often, but not always, comes first and adult men would usually be addressed by both names. Children are called by the personal name and it would be offensive if you used only a boy's religious name as his calling name. So, Muhammad Hamid Sheikh has a religious first name, a personal second and Sheikh is the family name. Girls are not given a religious name, so Hamid's sister is Razia Sheikh. Muslim families do not traditionally have a shared family name, but in Britain many have taken hereditary names denoting the family's social position or religious grouping, or have taken the father's personal name as a family surname.

▶ African naming systems are varied; it is a very large continent with many different ethnic groups. Some Hindus and Muslims come originally from Africa rather than Asia and there are differences in traditions. Many African cultural traditions place great store on the choice of name for a child. Names may be specially chosen to reflect the time and circumstances of a child's birth, joy at a baby's arrival or qualities of the child. It would be especially offensive if the name were changed by a worker who found it unfamiliar. African families do not traditionally have family surnames, although there is often a name that shows kinship. Many African families in Britain have taken a surname to ease everyday life.

Physical care

Good practice in work with children is a blend of attention to their care and learning needs. Care and health issues are not exactly the same across different ethnic and cultural groups. You will need to extend your existing experience when children come from groups with whom you are unfamiliar. Teams in mainly white areas may not have addressed their unspoken assumptions that children all need the same kind of care.

Black children need care routines for their hair and skin that differ from those of white children. African-Caribbean hair is a different texture to most white European hair. Children's (and adults') hair needs to be carefully combed and usually braided to avoid tangles and damage to the hair. Hair is conditioned and oiled, as is also common with Asian children.

Inexperienced workers can learn how to braid hair. It is a skill like any other and could be useful in braiding dolls' hair even if you do not have to style any individual child's hair. Make sure that you notice and admire children's hair especially if they have developed the idea that straight or fair hair is somehow better.

If black children get sand or grit into their hair, it is impossible to remove without redoing the style completely. So it is considerate to encourage children to wear a scarf or hat of their choice at the sand tray or in an outdoor sand pit. Obviously workers supervise and teach children not to throw any sand, but the material still tends to get into hair and clothes.

Black children's skin needs to be moisturised, otherwise it can become uncomfortably dry or cracked. Families use a range of ordinary, over the counter creams and lotions like coconut oil based preparations (not eczema medication). Ask parents what they use and you will probably find it will be a good hand and body lotion for everyone. You may not need to cream children unless you take the group swimming, in which case any white child with sensitive skin may also appreciate some lotion to counteract the dry itchy feeling that can be provoked by chlorinated water. Children may also need to cream their hands and lower arms if they have had a long session at the water tray. Black children's skin may be irritated by perfumed soaps and white children with sensitive skin may experience the same reaction, so unperfumed or basic baby soap will be best for everyone.

Such routines are not responses to special needs; they are ordinary, everyday needs for black children and undertaken by their families. The attention only seems 'special' if workers lack previous experience or are insisting on taking white European children as the benchmark for all care. Inexperienced white workers may also assume that black children are naturally protected against the sun, which is definitely not the case. The light skinned children will be in danger of burning more swiftly than their dark peers. However, black children will get sunburned and suffer from heat stroke, if adults are not properly vigilant in hot weather.

White children sometimes have differences in skin tone over their body, but such differences can be more obvious for black children. Children of African-Caribbean, Asian and Mediterranean origin sometimes have patches of darker skin that occur naturally and are called **Mongolian blue spots**. The darker skin can look like bruising to the inexperienced eye and these spots have led to some unjustified concerns about child protection. However, the natural darker areas are a consistent slate blue in colour, unlike genuine bruising that varies in shade and changes over a period of days.

Some issues about personal care arise because of religious reasons, some of which have become intertwined with cultural tradition. Modesty about undressing and other issues are discussed in Chapter 4 on page 137.

A range of families

Good practice in equal opportunities involves continually checking your assumptions about how families may operate, their relationship with your setting and the surrounding community. Some additional issues and concerns arise with two kinds of families which have not been covered so far in this chapter: travellers and refugee families.

Traveller families

There is a very long history of travelling families within Europe and many different theories about their origins. Travellers may have come originally from India or Egypt or may have their main roots in Ireland. A legal decision in 1988 ruled that Gypsies were a racial group within the meaning of the Race Relations Act 1976 (see also page 28) and that they are therefore covered by the legislation against discrimination. Families have been described as 'Gypsy' or 'Romany', but the term **traveller** is now the most usual word, since it describes how the families live and allows for different cultural and national backgrounds in the diverse population that travels from place to place within Britain.

Travellers frequently experience hostility and lack of understanding from the settled population. Poor relations are often provoked by the lack of proper sites on which travelling families can stop, despite the legal obligations of local authorities to provide such sites. Many travellers themselves have deep suspicions about the settled population (whom they call 'gaujos' or 'gorgios'). This wariness is sometimes fuelled by specific ill-treatment of their children in schools or general fears about the possible dangers experienced by traveller children when they are without the protection of their families.

ATTITUDES AND ASSUMPTIONS

Take the trouble to check out any assumptions and face the prejudices that you, your colleagues, other parents and the children may bring into your setting. Apart from any other negative views, you may find a tendency to divide travellers into 'real Gypsies' and more recent arrivals to the travelling life (for instance, new age travellers) who may be dismissed for a variety of reasons. Any verbal or physical bullying between children should be handled as you would any situation involving prejudiced behaviour. This is discussed on page 23. Questions from children, either of traveller or settled families, should be answered honestly, with the promise to find out when you do not know the answer.

Early years or school staff have sometimes been less than enthusiastic with traveller children because of the belief that the families will soon move on – 'So, what's the point?' This outlook is unacceptable for several reasons.

Families sometimes stay in one location for some time, or will return at a later date. Travellers who work as seasonal fruit pickers may well follow a similar circuit each year. You would not avoid making an effort for a child whose parents' professional commitments might move them on in the near future, so there is no justification for being less than fully attentive to traveller children. Even if families do move on, a positive experience for child and parent in your setting will support the whole family when they make a relationship with the next early years centre or school.

WELCOME AND RESOURCES

Settling into an early years centre or a school can be harder for travelling children than for even the most cautious children from settled families. Traveller children may not have previously experienced a large indoor space, especially one with the number of people and possible activities that can be found in some pre-schools or nurseries. Children who come to a nursery from living in a very small flat can sometimes feel similarly overwhelmed. Additionally, traveller children may not have encountered stairs, running water or flush lavatories. A sensitive early years worker can help by learning about the child's family experience to date and taking the time to show a child how unfamiliar indoor facilities work.

Good practice with traveller children has much in common with a positive approach in general to equal opportunities. You need to check your assumptions and be ready to learn about and from the children. For example:

▶ Traveller children will mostly share the English language with peers and staff in the setting, but the exact meaning of some words may vary in usage. For instance, traveller children may use the word 'bad' to mean 'ill', 'kushti' for 'good' or 'glaze' for glass.

▶ As a result of disrupted or very limited schooling in their own childhood, traveller parents may lack confidence in reading and writing or be illiterate. Adult illiteracy, or a limited ability to read and write, is a hidden problem for many adults. So, a sensitive approach to parents who seem to avoid written material will be useful for any families, not just traveller parents.

▶ Traveller children's play will of course reflect their particular experience. In the limited area of even a large caravan, children have to learn a careful use of space and avoid wastage of water. Different ways of cooking and storage will be reflected in their play in a home corner. Like any children, they will recreate their home.

▶ Although some traveller children have experience of a pre-school setting, for many the first day at primary school will be their very first time in a non-home environment with many strangers. If you work in a reception class, you may assume that children will have been to nursery or pre-school, because so many now do. Do not make this assumption for traveller children; they may well be new to the routines of group life in a school.

The early years tradition stresses that children learn through play. Although a valid point of view, this outlook can lead workers to undervalue what children learn from parents who deliberately teach them skills they will need in adult life. Early years workers and those in school need to respect and acknowledge the skills needed for travel and understand that traveller families traditionally regard childhood as an apprenticeship for adulthood, not as a stage apart from the rest of life. The children may be adept at skills which their settled peers only explore through pretend play. Children may be learning about the care of younger siblings, looking after animals or stripping down scrap material. Some travellers divide family work along clear cut gender lines, so you may find that the girls are learning about child care and other domestic tasks and the boys about dealing with scrap metal and working with horses. Some of the points made on page 35 about equal opportunities in relation to gender and cultural tradition may be important to bear in mind in partnership with traveller parents.

ACTIVITY

The view of traveller families that they will train children to be competent adults for their way of life is shared by families in a range of other cultural traditions. The importance of learning through play is an established professional tradition within British early years settings, but is not a universal approach. Gather your own thoughts and share ideas with colleagues, or fellow students on the following ideas:

▶ What can children learn at home with their parents (traveller or settled families) that they cannot easily learn within an early years setting?
▶ Children enjoy play and they learn, or extend their learning through play. But they also relish the opportunity to be properly involved in adult activities and to have a responsible role in the domestic routine. In what ways do you make such opportunities available in your setting?

If you have traveller children attending your setting, they should be able to see themselves in the play resources. If you do not currently work with traveller families, the situation might change in the future and some effort with your current group could help to promote positive attitudes. You could, for instance, explore the traveller way of life through themes of transport and different kinds of homes. A project on travel could highlight travelling as a way of life as well as looking at the short trips and holidays of settled families.

There are a relatively small number of books that feature traveller families:
The way we live series published by Hamish Hamilton includes *A traveller child* (1985) and *A circus child* (1986). Both of these books are written by Jose Patterson. They are out of print but try your local library.
The A&C Black *Strands* series includes *Gypsy family* by Mary Waterson (1978).
Rumer Godden *The diddakoi* (Puffin, 1975) is a story for older readers but you could read it in episodes to younger children.

Refugee families

The word refugee has a specific legal meaning under the 1951 UN Convention Relating to the Status of Refugees. Refugees are people who have left their own country and are unable to return 'owing to a well-founded fear of being persecuted for reasons of race, religion, nationality, membership of a particular social group or political opinion.' In order to stay in Britain, individuals or families who arrive as **asylum seekers** have to apply for **official refugee status**. During the 1990s asylum seekers in Britain came from such different countries as the former Yugoslavia, Sri Lanka, Turkey (Turkish Kurds), Somalia, Nigeria and Iraq.

The cultural, religious and linguistic background of refugee families will, of course, vary, because they come from different parts of the world. All of the good practice points discussed so far in this chapter will be relevant. Families may also have a home language other than English, so the points from page 114 will be relevant – children will be learning English as their second or third language. The routine and approach of an early years setting or a primary school may be anything from slightly to extremely unfamiliar to the children, depending on their country of origin.

In addition to becoming accustomed to a new country, refugee families will often have left their homes under distressing circumstances, and perhaps with very little chance to prepare the children. Adults and children may have traumatic memories of the disruptions that turned them into refugees. Even very young children may have seen terrible sights and know that members of their family, immediate or more extended, are still living or fighting in dangerous areas. Some children's family members may be missing or dead. The refugee families may be living in temporary accommodation with uncertainty about where they will live in the near future and whether the family will be allowed to stay in Britain. Support and understanding will be essential to help both the children and their parents.

You can consider using material about refugees to extend the understanding of all the children in your group, whether or not you ever have refugee children in your setting. Five- and six-year-olds can learn how, around the world, some children and their parents are given no choice about leaving their homes. The Save the Children Fund (see page 122 for address) has a range of posters and effective material using children's drawings and accounts like *One Day We Had to Run*.

Learning two or more languages

Bilingualism is common

It is estimated that about 70% of the world's population uses more than one language in everyday life. In countries of mainland Europe, confident use of two or more languages is normal for many people. In Britain there is a long history of bilingualism for speakers who have combined knowledge of English with fluency in Welsh, Scottish Gaelic (pronounced Gallic) and Irish Gaelic. Yet, until recent decades the common view in England was that the only 'normal' language development was for children to learn English and then to study one or more 'foreign' language at secondary school. The language movements in Wales and Scotland struggled against active attempts to suppress daily use of languages other than English. For instance, within the twentieth century some schools in Wales felt justified in caning children for speaking Welsh in ordinary conversation. So it is not really surprising that there was a very negative approach to minority ethnic families who became resident through immigration from the 1960s and whose first language was not English.

In the past, parents were told that they must speak only English to their children, otherwise the children's language development would be muddled. A fluent home language was often ignored and children's emerging English was treated as their only language, often leading to assessment of children as having 'poor' or 'no language'. A revision of views of good practice, combined with research about bilingual children, has led to a far more respectful approach and one that focuses properly on how children learn.

Children can learn to be bilingual in one of two ways:

1 **Simultaneous learning**: children learn two languages at the same time at home, when they are very young.
2 **Successive learning**: children, with a good grasp of their family language, learn a second language when they join an early years setting or school.

Helping bilingual children

SUPPORT PARENTS

You can support families in which children are able to speak two languages at the same time. Reassure any parents who have been told wrongly that they should only speak English. Young children can learn two languages simultaneously but, not surprisingly, they are helped when adults keep the two languages clearly distinguished. Perhaps one parent or another relative is consistently the person who speaks one language to the child, with the second language being consistently spoken by another member of the family. Children, do not learn so easily if adults switch language in mid-conversation or one parent joins in with their less fluent language. Children also need contact with child speakers of any language they speak, because children use language in a different way from adults.

HELPING CHILDREN

Many children are introduced to their second language in early years settings or when they go to school (successive learning). Young children do not just pick up a second language; they need and benefit from adult help. Ideally, children who are learning a second language in an early years setting need a day or session that is initially run in the child's most fluent language, then the second language, English, is introduced. This approach may not be possible in your setting, because you do not have fluent adult speakers of the child's home language or perhaps many languages are represented. You need to make the most of children's settling-in period at your centre and be ready to learn from the parent or carer who stays with the child.

ENCOURAGE FRIENDSHIPS

Children flourish through social contact with other children and you will support bilingual children by encouraging their friendships. In a supportive atmosphere, young children will make friendships across language boundaries and they are creative in using non-verbal communication and a few shared words to extend play.

Children who share the same home language can support each other and it can be a great relief to children to talk with ease to someone else. You will understand this feeling if you have ever lived or worked somewhere where few people spoke your own first language. Workers should never give children a hard time for speaking a language other than English to each other. You can reasonably ask children to tell or show you what is absorbing them, so that you or other children can join an activity or conversation.

Specific Adult Help

Remember that three- and four-year-olds learning their second language in nursery or playgroup have come a long way since they learned their first language at home. So, do not treat them as if they were very young children. They have many ideas and a breadth of understanding. They just cannot yet express themselves in a language that you and they share. There are many ways in which you can help children learn a second language:

▶ Encourage children's whole communication. They need to feel comfortable to use plenty of non-verbal communication, as well as the words and phrases they have learned so far.

▶ Listen to what a child is telling you, sometimes with creative combinations that communicate their meaning. You should speak clearly and in simple phrases to children but otherwise talk as you would to any child of their age.

▶ Children need to be in a setting that encourages them to start talking and not worry overmuch about correct forms until they have plenty of the second language with which to work.

▶ Children will assume that the language they hear is directly relevant to what they can see in front of them. So you can help by making sure that you link your phrases and short sentences in an obvious way to play activities, people, objects or events.

▶ Keep talking with children in a direct way that involves them in activities and the routine of your setting. Do not worry if a child is silent initially. Some children prefer to wait to speak the new language until they have a reasonable number of words and phrases.

▶ Be aware that, if children have started to learn a written language, they may be familiar with a different alphabet from English and in some cases to writing in the opposite direction to the European way. Arabic, for instance, is written from right to left.

▶ Be ready to learn some key phrases of greeting and comfort in a child's most fluent language. Encourage the children to greet each other using the languages spoken in your setting.

▶ Partnership with parents will be crucial. Where you share a fluent language with parents, they can be invaluable in explaining ideas to a child in his or her first language, easing the transfer to English and helping children to use a vocabulary that is small at the moment. If you and the parent do not share a language, then you will sometimes need the services of an interpreter. This person may be a bilingual colleague or another parent, so long as the first parent is happy with this arrangement.

ACTIVITY

Young children who are becoming bilingual are not in the same position as babies and toddlers learning a first language. Very young children start to learn the names of people and objects, but a three-year-old bilingual child is intellectually beyond naming and needs phrases as well as words.

▶ Listen in to your daily talk with children. Are there words and phrases that arise a great deal during the day or session? It may help if you make clear use of phrases like 'would you like a . . .' or 'Please give me the . . .'.

▶ Do not forget the importance of gesture and other kinds of non-verbal communication. Children learning a second language will be helped by clear gestures as well as supported by non-verbal encouragement such as smiles and enthusiastic nods.

A positive approach to languages

RESPECT

In an early years, playwork or school setting you should show that you respect the languages that all children speak and any different versions of English or accents. If adults show respect, then children will follow. Activities can also be used to broaden children's horizons and to build an understanding that there are languages other than their own home language.

You should step in if any children try out languages or accents in a mocking way, caricaturing speech that they do not understand. In school, children may be ridiculed about their accent, whether this is a different version of English or a non-local accent. If you talk and listen to the children, you may conclude that some harassment is racist and deal with the incident accordingly. But early years and school workers should recognise that any children can be tormented over their accent. I have certainly known some middle-class children (white and black) mercilessly bullied for having a 'posh' accent by children (also white and black), whose social background was more working class.

ACTIVITIES

There is a good range of dual language books which can be supportive for bilingual children, but equally valuable for monolingual children who are discovering that the whole world does not share their spoken and written language. You can buy tapes of stories, songs and rhymes in different languages. Or you may be fortunate in having bilingual workers or parents who could make a tape for your group.

Even in an apparently non-diverse area, there will be workers, parents or grandparents who have a second language. In mainly white areas, there may well be families whose origins are Irish, Polish, German or some other mainland European country. Some adults will have a second language that they learned in school. They may be rusty, but willing to share their knowledge with the children, who are not after all going to grade them on their accent or grammar.

Children may giggle at first, especially if the unknown language is spoken by someone from whom they have previously only heard English. (I can recall my own children at three and five years being convulsed with laughter when I ordered our meal in French on the family's first trip to France.) You can acknowledge that hearing a new language from a known adult seems odd at the start, but stress that the language is real and perhaps Somali or Italian children would find English very amusing at the first time of hearing.

ACTIVITY

Make a chart of the languages and accents represented in your own setting. What is spoken by children, workers, parents and other family members? You could extend the activity by adding languages and accents that can be heard locally, but are not represented in the setting at the moment. You might also include a historical element – how has the area changed in recent decades or over the twentieth century? For instance:

▶ In the 1950s, Bedford had a sizeable arrival of Italian workers for the brick factories.
▶ In my own local area of south London there is a Polish population dating from the second world war – enough people to support a Polish Catholic church and Polish can be heard on the streets, spoken by older residents.

▶ If you are in or near the West country, then you could explore the history of Cornish. This language exists in a written form but people who wish to revive spoken Cornish have not always agreed on how to say the words.

All children will bring their family experience into their play

You could alert children to different written forms of language. Some bilingual families may be able to help you in displays of languages that use different alphabets and forms of writing. In school, you may be fortunate that some children can actually demonstrate writing in their home language. You can buy multilingual Welcome notices. However, it would be worth developing one of your own, that draws on the languages spoken or understood by the families who actually attend your setting.

Further resources

Books

Arnberg, Leonora (1987) *Raising Children Bilingually: the pre-school years* (Multilingual Matters)
Written for parents but with ideas for anyone who works with children.

Epstein, Debbie and Sealey, Alison (1990) *Where it Really Matters – developing anti-racist education in predominantly white primary schools* (Development Education Centre, see address on page 192)
Practical ideas and discussion about an effective approach where there is little apparent local diversity.

Jay, Eric (1992) *Keep Them in Birmingham – challenging racism in south-west England* (Commission for Racial Equality)
Report of a project based in the West Country, where there is little apparent ethnic diversity, although a past history of black residents.

Lane, Jane (1989) *The Playgroup/Nursery* in Cole, Mike (ed) *Education for Equality: some guidelines for practice* (Routledge)
Discussion about why a positive approach to racial equality matters in early years.

Lane, Jane (1996) *From Cradle to School: a practical guide to racial equality in early childhood education and care* (Commission for Racial Equality)
Explains how the Race Relations Act 1976 and the Children Act 1989 apply to early years work. Suggestions about good practice and training.

Milner, David (1983) *Children and Race: ten years on* (Ward Lock Educational)
Discussion of the research about children's attitudes and some practical and social issues. The 'ten years on' refers to the time passed since the first edition of the book in 1973.

Paley, Vivian Gussin (1979) *White Teacher* (Harvard University Press)
Description and reflection on what happened in Paley's classroom and how she learned about racial issues from the perspective of black children.

Rutter, Jill (1994) *Refugee Children in the Classroom* (Trentham Books)
Discussion of the special issues raised by refugee children who, as well as a wealth of ethnic and cultural backgrounds, may bring the results of traumatic experiences. A short booklet (undated) *Helping Refugee Children in Schools* is available from The Refugee Council (see address on page 122).

Siraj-Blatchford, Iram (1994) *The Early Years: laying the foundations for racial equality* (Trentham Books)

Research, policy and practice for people working with under-eights.

Save the Children (1991) *Playing in Harmony: an early years resource pack* (Save the Children Scotland)
Practical information on cultural diversity and work with children.

Slater, Mary (1993) *Health for All Our Children: achieving appropriate health care for black and minority ethnic children and their families* (Action for Sick Children)
Practical ways in which health services need to address cultural traditions and everyday needs in health care, hygiene and diet.

Smikle, Jacqueline, Moynihan, Clare and des Vignes, Liz-anne (1997) *One Vision: cultural awareness pack* (Save the Children)
Report of a project to extend children's cultural awareness in one London centre. The work was linked with desirable learning outcomes.

Tizard, Barbara and Phoenix, Ann (1993) *Black, White or Mixed-race: race and racism in the lives of young people with mixed parentage* (Routledge)
Report of research that gives equal space to the children's perspective as well as adult views on the experience of mixed parentage.

Troyna, Barry and Hatcher, Richard (1992) *Racism in Children's Lives: a study of mainly white primary schools* (Routledge/National Children's Bureau)
Research into the behaviour and attitudes of children which highlights the issues in an effective anti-racist policy.

Wright, Cecile (1992) *Race Relations in the Primary School* (David Fulton)
Descriptive study of four inner city primary schools which explores experiences of black children and examples of differential treatment by teachers.

Zealey, Caroline (1995) *The Importance of Names* in *The Coordinate Collection on Equal Opportunities* (National Early Years Network)
Caroline Zealey gives details on cultural traditions in names. The collection includes other useful articles.

Many authors (1996) *Making it Real: introducing a global dimension in the early years* (Development Education Centre/Community Education Development Centre/Save the Children)
Ways of introducing young children to the wide range of traditions and life styles around the world.

The journal *Multicultural Teaching* often has useful articles. It is available from Trentham Books, Westview House, 734 London Road, Oakhill, Stoke-on-Trent ST4 5NP Tel: 01782 745567

Organisations

Commission for Racial Equality, Head Office, Elliot House, 10–12 Allington Street, London SW1E 5EH Tel: 0171 828 7022

Aims to promote equality of opportunity and to monitor the Race Relations Act 1976. There are some regional offices in addition to the Head Office. The CRE publishes books and some posters. The publications are handled by Central Books, 99 Wallis Road, London E9 5LN Tel: 0181 986 4854.

Early Years Anti-Racist Network (EYTARN) PO Box 28, Wallasey L45 9NP Tel: 0151 639 6136

Produces booklets, some posters and other illustrations, and runs training workshops and conferences.

Save the Children Fund, Information Officer (Travellers) 17 Grove Lane, London SE5 8RD Tel: 0171 703 5400

SCF has links with projects on traveller families and children as well as working in many other areas.

The Refugee Council, Bondway House, 3 Bondway, London SW8 1SJ Tel: 0171 582 6922

The council offers services to refugee families, advice and training and a range of publications.

Working Group Against Racism in Children's Resources (WGARCR), 460 Wandsworth Road, London SW8 3LX Tel: 0171 627 4594

Publishes booklets and resources lists, runs workshops and publishes guidelines on evaluating play materials and books.

See also the list of organisations and suppliers from page 192.

4

World religions – respect and knowledge

A note on spelling

The world religions covered in this chapter do not all share the same language, written script or alphabet. Decisions about how to translate and spell religious terms have therefore led to variations. The Muslim festival of Id-ul-Fitr is sometimes spelled as Eid-ul-Fitr. The Hindu and Sikh festival of Divali also appears as Diwali. The Jewish festival of Hanukkah can be spelled as Chanukah.

For consistency I have followed the spelling given in *Religious Education: glossary of terms* (published by the School Curriculum and Assessment Authority in 1994). This glossary was produced in consultation with all the relevant faith communities.

Religious belief and practice

Knowledge and understanding

You are not expected to be an expert on all the major world religions. But your responsibility in good practice is to be aware of the gaps in what you know and to be ready to learn more. You also need to be open to checking your understanding and questioning any assumptions that you may share with colleagues. In the past, you may have misunderstood the real significance of a religious festival or the reason for particular practices.

If you keep an open mind, you will extend your learning about faiths that are unfamiliar to you. But you are also likely to learn more about the religious faith that is most familiar to you, perhaps a faith in which you were raised or which you still practise. It can be hard to stand back from beliefs that seem very ordinary, part of everyday life, but it can be valuable to grasp finally, the source of certain traditions. This opportunity to continue learning applies whatever the faith that is most familiar to you.

Respect and belief

ADULT ATTITUDES

You will not be in tune with everyone over religious belief or philosophies about lifestyle. You are not expected to agree, or pretend to agree with every colleague or parent who expresses their clear beliefs. Good practice will be to:

▶ Have a clear policy on equal opportunities as it affects matters of faith. Workers in every setting need opportunities to discuss within the team any confusions or disagreements that arise through conversations with parents, or indeed from lack of agreement within the team.

▶ Acknowledge differences and show respect for beliefs and practices that you may not share. This respect is important regardless of whether you currently have a family attending the setting who follow the faith in question.

▶ Recognise that parents who do not actively follow a particular faith can still have strong beliefs about how to behave and raise their children. It is disrespectful to assume that families with no specific religious beliefs will have no moral values that guide their decisions.

▶ Show respect through an active attempt to understand any requests that parents make based on religious beliefs. If the setting genuinely cannot meet parents' requests, then you should be honest and seek a compromise, if possible.

▶ Ensure the range of activities and celebrations in your setting shows that you value all world faiths and that you are not behaving as if one religion is more important than any other.

UNCOMPROMISING BELIEFS

It is undoubtedly the case that some people with strongly held religious beliefs think that they are definitely right, and anyone who does not share their beliefs is definitely wrong. Most of the major world religions have followers who take this view, and some groups within each faith are more dogmatic than others. This situation can complicate good practice on equal opportunities. Respect for anyone's beliefs has to be balanced with an awareness that nobody is to impose their beliefs on others in the setting.

If your setting has no definite religious affiliation, then any parent, worker or volunteer needs to understand the equal opportunities policy in practice. Everyone has a right to their own beliefs, and the setting will show respect and attempt to be flexible over any religious practice requests. However, with that right comes a responsibility – to show respect for others and not to tell the children that only the one faith is true or sensible.

Some nurseries, playgroups or pre-schools are linked with a specific place of worship and particular religious faith. So long as they have to be registered under the Children Act 1989, these settings are still obliged to show respect for religions other than the faith followed by the staff. It is also required that the setting makes the religious affiliation clear on any material that is published about the setting. Local registration and inspection officers have been faced with a dilemma over early years groups with a single and strong religious affiliation. On the one hand, the practice in such groups is unlikely to show an active respect for the religious beliefs of families who do not share the preferred faith. On the other hand, the requirements of the Children Act are not specific enough to refuse to register such a group, when other standards of good practice are met.

This area is one where there are no easy answers. I have chosen to organise this chapter around the moral stance that any early years, school or playwork setting should show an active respect for all faiths, and that neither workers nor volunteers should promote a view that one faith is absolutely right and another is wrong. The perspective of the chapter is consistent with equal opportunities policies, but I recognise that complex issues can arise in putting such policies into practice.

CHILDREN'S LEARNING

You are helping children to learn in many different areas and they will continue to learn into the future. Sometimes workers are concerned, 'Are we expected to tell young children everything about religion?' The answer to this question has to be 'No'. You are starting a process of knowledge and developing understanding that will continue. You are opening possibilities for children when you introduce ideas and give them a range of experiences relevant to different faiths.

This approach has much in common with other areas of your work with children. For instance, you are not trying to tell and show a four-year-old everything there is to know about mathematical understanding, or scientific investigations. You are introducing basic ideas, encouraging children to explore through doing and asking questions and hopefully stimulating an interest in what will later become a larger area of knowledge.

If you are working in a school setting, then your approach to the curriculum will be guided by the Education Reform Act 1988. This legislation stated that any syllabus for religious education should reflect the fact that religious traditions in Britain are mainly Christian, while taking account of the other principal religions represented in the country. This general guidance has been interpreted differently in schools, depending partly on the beliefs represented in the local community.

If you work in a diverse area, you may have children attending your setting whose families follow a number of different world religions. Families may be able and willing to support activities in the setting, but you should not restrict yourself only to those faiths that are represented in your current group. Your aim is to extend the learning of all the children.

Young children are developing their views on moral and spiritual issues just as they are learning attitudes about other aspects of social relationships and how people should behave. Workers should not tell children what they should believe. However, making information available to children is not the same as indoctrinating them. Children will learn attitudes towards different faiths and religious practices whether adults believe they are influencing children or not. A setting that makes no efforts beyond celebrating what the staff view as the 'normal' festivals from only one faith, is effectively telling the children that this faith is the one that matters.

Religion and culture

Religious beliefs and practices have shaped societies around the world. When there has been a long history of a particular faith associated with a country, then religious practices become merged with the culture and can affect virtually every aspect of a society: social, moral and political. What was originally rooted in religious faith becomes part of 'normal' life. Habits are absorbed into everyday language, expected ways of behaving and celebrations by people who are no longer active members of the religious faith.

The merging of religious and cultural tradition is fascinating if you are interested in history, but it is also very relevant to understand as an early years or playworker. Parents may make a request over, for instance, diet for their child but conversation leads you to realise that the parents are not actively religious. You should still respect their request. Even adults who no longer practise the faith in which they were raised, may still feel uncomfortable about foods that are not allowed for religious reasons. The impact of religion on cultural tradition will be strong within your own culture. But you will probably not be aware of it, unless you have explored your assumptions about what is 'normal'.

Some dance and music has religious as well as cultural traditions

England as an Example

English society has a long history of being shaped by Christianity. The Church of England is the established church and for a long time being 'C of E' was regarded by many people as much the same as being 'English'. Of course, there were, and are, different groups within Christianity and England is not the only country in Britain. I recall as a child visiting the Welsh half of my family and being kindly corrected by my grandmother, who explained that in the valleys people did not go to church, they went to chapel. The Church of England was the English faith and the local community was Welsh Methodist by tradition.

In November 1997, the Archbishop of Canterbury, George Carey, publicly expressed his disagreement with inter-faith worship in Britain. He was quoted as saying, 'Other faiths comprise less than 10% of the population. So, 90% are still rooted in a Christian position.' (Interview for the magazine *Third Way*.) Of course, 90% of the population are not regular church attenders, but Dr Carey felt justified in counting as nominally Christian, anyone in Britain who had not actively committed to another faith.

You may find an unquestioned assumption within your team that families will be Christian unless they definitely say otherwise. I am not the only parent to have left a deliberate blank in the space asking for family religion in their child's school information sheet, only to find later that someone in the school office had filled in 'Christian' without further consultation.

Other common beliefs or preferences are also associated with the strong Christian influence on British cultural tradition. For instance:

▶ The use of the phrase 'Christian' name for someone's personal, rather than family name, arises from the religious tradition of christening babies within Protestant and Catholic forms of Christianity.
▶ Religious ceremonies of christening, marriage and funeral services have been to a great extent absorbed into cultural traditions. People who could not be described as active members of the local church often still wish to be married in church, possibly have their children christened and assume that a priest will conduct their funeral service. These events feel like the right way to behave and to celebrate significant life events.
▶ Assumptions rooted in cultural tradition are sometimes supported by reference to the Bible, and sometimes in misquotation. Phrases from the Old or New Testament are sometimes quoted as justification for taking revenge on wrongdoers, why people should eat meat and not be vegetarians or as a justification for hitting young children.

TO THINK ABOUT

If your childhood was in Britain, or another culture strongly influenced by Christianity, you may never have questioned a feeling that it is normal to believe in one God (**monotheism**) and that religions that have more than one deity are therefore strange. You may make other, similar assumptions.

I recall working with an early years team which included white and African-Caribbean workers as well as one Asian worker. Most of the team had a Christian background, even if they were no longer active. Conversation turned to Hinduism during one session and several people turned to their Asian colleague to say with great surprise, 'But *you* don't believe in reincarnation, do you?' She replied, 'Of course I do.' The group clearly had to adjust to the experience that someone, who was very much 'one of us', believed in an idea that they had learned was odd.

Major world religions

Diversity within a faith

You may be aware of the variety of beliefs and sub-groups within the world faith that you know best, but diversity is a feature of every major world faith. There is nothing like complete agreement on beliefs, interpretations of the main holy book(s), the details of everyday practice like diet and dress, or on the many other aspects of religious activity and related cultural tradition.

All the major world religions have spread beyond their point of origin, either because of population movements or because practitioners of the faith have deliberately set out to convert people from other cultures. Some religions have developed variations in different locations, sometimes because they have absorbed the practices of pre-existing religions in the culture or because of unresolved divisions within the faith. The Orthodox Church in Eastern Europe split over questions of belief from Christianity as it developed in western Europe. Buddhism in India differs from Japanese Buddhism which developed in co-existence with Shintoism, an ancient religion based in animist beliefs of a supernatural force within all natural objects.

Within every major faith there are sub-groups, some of whom disagree strongly, even violently, about the details of beliefs. For no faith can you confidently say 'everyone believes that . . .' or 'everyone behaves in this way'. Nor should you generalise from the behaviour of the more uncompromising groups that exist within most faiths, to say that all followers of that religion are intolerant of others. Divisions between followers of different faiths (Hindus and Muslims in India) or between different versions of the same religion (Protestant and Catholic in Northern Ireland) can become entangled in historical, political and social factors. The result can be severe disruption within the society which is very hard to counteract.

Buddhism

This ancient religion stretches back some 2500 years and has its origins in India. Gautama, the founder of Buddhism, was a prince who was born to wealth and comfort but decided that he had to come to terms with the suffering in life. His search for learning led him to decide on a 'middle way' between self-indulgence and self-denial. During a night in May when the moon was full, Gautama went into a state of deep meditation and emerged the following morning as the Buddha, which means 'The Enlightened One'.

He continued for many years as a teacher and Buddhism as a faith spread beyond India.

The Pali Canon (Pali is an ancient Asian language) is a collection of Buddhist scriptures that are learned by monks so that they can be recited during festivals. Meditation is very important within Buddhism because it is through this process that it is possible to attain an inner calm and mental clarity. Buddhists do not believe in god(s) but in following the right way of life as laid out by the Buddha. This is defined by the Eightfold Path which covers actions towards others as well as a focus on the search for truth and understanding.

Buddhists believe in reincarnation: that people die but are reborn into another life. The nature of their new life is dependent on their behaviour in previous lives. People who strive to lead a blameless existence will become so pure that they achieve Nirvana, a state that takes them out of the cycle of death and rebirth.

Christianity

The Christian faith includes many sub-groups who share some beliefs, while differing over other aspects of religious dogma or practice. Christians share a belief in one God who created the world and in the human form of God in Jesus Christ (the Messiah) who was born to a Jewish family and lived in Palestine about 2000 years ago.

Christians are monotheistic: worshipping the one God. But some groups, for instance Catholics, place a stronger emphasis than others on the importance of Christ's mother, the Virgin Mary, and different saints (men and women who have led such a blameless life that they are deemed to reach a state of sainthood). Christ represents the ideal of a selfless person who championed poor and oppressed people and who died in order to take the sins of humankind upon himself. Christians believe that Christ rose from death three days after his crucifixion and continued to appear to his disciples for a further 40 days. The early Christians were Jews, but the faith was soon taken to non-Jewish communities and cultures.

The main Christian holy book is the Bible, which is in two parts. The Old Testament is shared with Judaism but is interpreted differently: Christians believe it predicts the birth of Christ, whereas Jews believe the Messiah is yet to come. The New Testament is specific to Christianity in that it tells the life of Christ and his followers as the Christian faith was spread around the Middle East and Mediterranean. Some Christians, for instance, fundamentalist groups and Jehovah's Witnesses, believe the Bible to be literally true in every word, whereas other Christian groups regard the content as more open to interpretation. Christians believe that there is only one life and that after death believers are united with God in heaven. Some groups are more certain than others that unbelievers will go to hell, a place of torment and suffering.

Hinduism

This religious tradition is one of the oldest world faiths and appears to have become established about 5000 years ago. The name 'Hinduism' is more recent and dates from about 800 years ago, when Muslims invading India wanted to distinguish the existing religion from Islam. Hindu was the Persian word for Indian.

The traditional holy texts in Hinduism are the four Vedas, which are written in the ancient language of Sanskrit, now spoken only by scholars. Hindus believe in a supreme being whose different aspects are manifested in many devas, each of whom possess specific individual powers and may appear in human or animal form. For instance, Lakshmi represents wealth and prosperity, whereas Ganesh is the deva who is able to remove obstacles in the lives of those who worship him. Different Hindu festivals usually feature different individual devas.

Hindus believe in reincarnation: that souls are reborn in an everlasting cycle in which the quality of one's current life is affected by behaviour in previous lives (the concept of karma). The concept of samsara describes the flow of life from birth to death and then to rebirth in a continuing process. The traditional Hindu social system appears originally to have been determined by the talents shown by individuals. However, it developed into an inflexible caste system by which individuals' place in society was determined by the family into which they were born. The Buddha (see Buddhism earlier in the section) specifically rejected the caste system and, during the twentieth century, development in India has included an attempt to return to a more flexible system of social positioning.

Islam

Islam developed as a world faith about 1400 years ago. Muhammad was a respected and prosperous merchant in Mecca who reached a point of personal crisis. He sought the loneliness of the desert to find some answers. During that experience, Muhammad had visions which convinced him he had been called upon by the angel Gabriel to be the prophet of the one God (Allah). Muhammad continued to receive revelations from Allah and these are contained in the sacred book of Islam, the Qur'an.

The term Islam means the peace attained through a willing obedience to Allah's divine guidance. Followers of the faith are known as Muslims. Muslims accept Islam by making a declaration of faith (the Shahadah): 'There is no god except Allah, Muhammad is the Messenger of Allah.' Muslims believe that there is one life only and that Allah will judge people according to their behaviour and assign them to heaven or hell. Muslims believe that Muhammad was the final Prophet in the chain of communication between Allah and humankind. Abraham, Moses, other important figures from Jewish early history and the Old Testament, and Jesus Christ were earlier Prophets who should be respected. Unlike Christians, Muslims do not believe that Christ was the Son of God.

The Shari'ah forms the details of Islamic law and is based on the Qur'an and other writings describing the example set by the Prophet Muhammad. Interpretations of the Shari'ah vary and some Muslim communities are considerably stricter than others.

Judaism

Judaism has existed for about 3500 years. Jews believe in one God who created the world and chose the Jewish people to be an example to all humankind. Jews believe that God communicated a moral code through prophets and this guidance is set out in the Torah. This holy book includes the first five books of what is known to Christians as the Old Testament.

Jews believe that we have only one life and should obey God's laws within that life. Orthodox Jews aim to follow in detail all the requirements of the Torah, but other Jewish groups, for instance Reform Jews, believe that the guidance is open to interpretation for life in a changing society. The laws covered by the Torah include the Ten Commandments, believed (by Jews and Christians) to have been given by God to the prophet Moses.

Jews worship in the synagogue, but the family home is also an important focus for religious observance. The holy day, the Sabbath, is celebrated every week at home through preparations including cleaning the home and wearing fresh clothes, making blessings and prayers, and eating a family meal. The Sabbath lasts for 25 hours from sunset on Friday evening until the stars shine in the night sky on Saturday.

Sikhism

The Sikh faith developed over 500 years ago within the Punjab (an area now in both Pakistan and north-west India). The movement was started by the Guru Nanak and continued by nine subsequent gurus (teachers). Sikhs believe in one God, who is the true Guru, and whose divine word was communicated through the ten gurus. The sacred collection of Sikh scriptures is called the Guru Granth Sahib.

Sikhs believe that the tenth guru, Guru Gobind Singh, transferred his authority to the community and so there was no further need for an individual guru. There was an attempt to leave behind the Hindu caste system and the naming that reflected caste. Men were therefore given the name of Singh (lion) and women that of Kaur (princess).

Sikhs believe that, as people become more aware of God, their lives will change away from selfishness. Sikhs worship at the gurdwara (meaning the guru's door). They do not have formal priests, but some people are specially trained to read and explain the Guru Granth Sahib. Sikhs believe in reincarnation and that only a few people will leave the cycle of death and rebirth by finding a true union with God.

Beliefs and personal care

Partnership with parents

Some specific issues arise over religious belief and cultural traditions:

▶ The written material on your setting and early conversations with parents should make clear in what way your setting approaches religious belief and the celebration of festivals.
▶ Be ready to answer any questions or doubts raised by the parents about what you do in your setting, how you do it and why.
▶ Along with the other information that you are courteously gathering from parents, you need to know whether the family has a definite religious affiliation. You also need to know, and show parents that you will respect their wishes, whether the family's beliefs lead to specific requests about their child.

▶ If you are unclear what the parents are asking, or about activities about which they have reservations, then ask. Once you understand a parent's request, then you can make an honest commitment to follow what they want, or explain why their request causes you some difficulty.

Food and drink

A number of world religions have a tradition of giving thanks for food, either at most mealtimes or on specific occasions. An early years or school setting may also have a tradition of giving thanks, but this can be a general appreciation for food and not a specifically Christian way of 'saying grace'.

Any setting should ask parents about what their children eat, or do not eat. (Some children have allergies to certain foodstuffs and these must be avoided.) Some families will request that their children are not given particular food or drink because these are unacceptable for religious reasons. Some families may also follow a particular diet, perhaps be vegetarian, for philosophical reasons. Some general guidelines follow, but please recall the earlier comment that there is a great deal of variety within every faith. You will always need to talk with the parents, and with the children when they are old enough to explain to you.

BUDDHISM

Buddhists are sometimes vegetarian, but not always. For any children who are vegetarian, you need to get into the habit of checking the ingredients of processed and convenience foods. Some products surprisingly include meat-derived ingredients, such as gelatine or rennet. There are vegetarian alternatives to both. Some cheap ice creams include animal fat.

CHRISTIANITY

Most Christians do not follow particular rules for their diet, although some make a case against vegetarianism by quoting the Bible. However, a few Christian groups do avoid certain foods.

Jehovah's Witnesses require that meat has been specially bled during slaughter and avoid foods like black pudding because of the blood. Mormons avoid black pudding and caffeine in any form, so children should not have cola drinks. Some Rastafarians follow a vegetarian diet close to vegan – avoiding dairy products. If Rastafarian families eat meat, they will probably avoid pork and shellfish. (The Rastafarian faith is a blend of Biblical teachings and African cultural traditions.)

Hinduism

Some Hindus are vegetarian, but those who eat meat will avoid any beef and beef products, since cows are regarded as sacred.

Judaism

The laws of Kashrut determine the foods that can be eaten and those that are forbidden, the method of slaughter of animals and the preparation of food. Permitted foods (Kosher, meaning allowed) include animals with a cloven hoof, birds that are not predators and fish with fins. Meat and poultry must be obtained from Kosher butchers, because animals have to be slaughtered in such a way that all the blood drains out of the bodies. The meat is then blessed by the Rabbi (the religious leader of the local synagogue). Meat and dairy products should be kept completely separate at all stages of food preparation, serving and eating and in washing up afterwards.

Jewish families vary in how closely they observe the laws of Kashrut. Orthodox families will be the strictest, but their children will almost certainly attend Jewish early years settings. It is impossible to offer proper Kosher food unless you have a kitchen organised along Kosher lines, which means two sets of cutlery, crockery and dish washing facilities. Often the only option for children from an Orthodox family attending a non-Jewish setting, will be to bring a packed lunch. Less strict Jewish families will ask that their children are not given pork in any form, nor shellfish.

Muslim

Muslim families avoid pork in any form. As with meals for Jewish children, you have to watch out for unexpected pork products in processed foods and read the list of ingredients carefully. Any meat or poultry must be Halal (meaning lawful) which is produced by a method of slaughter that allows the body to bleed. The meat or poultry is dedicated to Allah by the Imam (the religious leader of the local mosque).

Sikh

Some Sikhs are vegetarian, but those who eat meat will probably avoid beef and pork. Families will want meat from a butcher that has **not** been bled in the Halal or Kosher method.

Good Practice

Any requests from families about food and drink for their children should be handled with respect and communicated to all the staff who will have contact with children. Good patterns of communication can be especially important in schools where teachers may have the conversation with parents, but support staff supervise mealtimes. If your early years setting is in a diverse area, then one very practical approach is to ensure that children always have a proper vegetarian option for every mealtime.

You may find yourself in an awkward position if children do not want to follow their family's diet, perhaps because they want to eat the same meal as a close friend. You should talk with a child to ensure that he or she understands the ingredients of the meal and that his or her parents would rather they took an alternative meal. It is a difficult issue but then you probably have to leave the decision to the child, especially if older. Make sure that neither the other children or workers are creating an atmosphere at mealtimes that makes the child feel uncomfortable about following the family diet.

Food preferences and traditions vary considerably and no workers should take the line that one tradition is the normal way of eating and any variation is odd or a fad. Some people may claim that they eat anything and that other people have a restricted diet but this is usually untrue. For instance, English people who happily eat meat are not usually willing to eat every edible animal, bird or fish. Some mainland European countries regard the English habit of eating lamb with much the same distaste that many English people view eating horse meat.

Fasting

Giving up foods at particular times or fasting for periods is part of religious practice in some faiths.

CHRISTIANITY

Fasting or giving up particular foods used to be common practice within the Christian faith. Some Christians still avoid meat on Fridays (the day of the death of Christ) and some give up one or two foods for Lent (the forty days leading up to Easter), usually a food that is something of a treat, like sugar in coffee or sweets. Catholics may fast on Ash Wednesday, the first day of Lent. Christians from the Orthodox Church are more likely to follow the religious tradition of avoiding meat, eggs and milk products for all of Lent.

JUDAISM

Jewish families will fast from the evening before Yom Kippur (the Day of Atonement) until the following nightfall. Yom Kippur is the tenth day after Rosh Hashanah (the Jewish New Year that falls in September) and is an important time when the sins of the past year are recalled and forgiveness is asked.

Islam

You are most likely to encounter fasting if you work with children from Muslim families, who will fast during Ramadan. This important part of the Muslim faith falls within the ninth month of the Muslim year. Since the Islamic year is based on the lunar calendar, the exact date of Ramadan varies and, according to Western dates, will be 'earlier' each year (see page 139 for an explanation of the different calendars and festival dates). Ramadan starts with the first sighting of the new moon and lasts for the lunar month. Muslims fast from dawn until sunset during Ramadan as a means of focusing on spiritual standards. Ramadan is complete at Id-ul-Fitr. Id means the end of fasting and a religious celebration.

Fasting during the daylight hours of Ramadan is very important for Muslims and should be respected. Families are careful about bringing children into the tradition, so it is not until puberty that young people will join adults in fasting completely from food or drink. If you work in a school or after school club, then you should be aware that children may be joining the fast for some days or for a few hours within the day. In all settings, children may be more tired than usual, because they will have risen to join their family in the pre-dawn meal. They may benefit from quieter activities and a chance to sit in the shade when Ramadan falls within the summer. Children may also want a quiet room for prayer so you should talk with the parents about their needs.

Clothing and hair

Some faiths have requirements about clothing which arise from considerations of modesty and religious tradition. Muslim families may be concerned that girls keep their hair and legs covered. As in any faith, some families will be stricter about their children's dress code than others. Problems arise if workers are insensitive to arrangements over changing for games, what children wear for physical activities or if staff insist on swimming for all children.

You should be ready to consider children's dignity and wish for privacy, regardless of whether specific religious views have been expressed. Adults often think that children will not mind communal changing rooms, or even changing in the primary school corridor. But some children seriously dislike the lack of privacy and some object to being expected to do games or dance in their underwear, if that is the school's practice with younger children. You can ensure that all children have options.

Children may sometimes wear items that have religious significance. Good practice is to ask parents and certainly not to insist on removal of an item just because it looks unimportant to you. For instance, some children of Christian families may wear a small crucifix on a chain around the neck. Chinese children may wear charms that are associated with good fortune. Hindu boys may wear a plaited red and gold bracelet (Rakhi) at the festival of Raksha Bandhan as a pledge to protect their sister or a close friend to whom they will act as a brother. Sikh children may wear a steel band (Kara) on the right wrist, which is of great importance as one of the five 'K's, symbols of the faith worn by Sikhs.

Several faiths have traditions about covering the head and hair.

▶ Muslim girls may have a scarf pulled over the head or a full head covering which frames the face.
▶ Some Jewish and Christian groups require women and girls to keep their head covered by a scarf, although all the hair may not have to be enclosed.
▶ Jewish boys from some families will wear a kippa, the skull cap.
▶ Rastafarian parents may ask that their daughters keep their hair neatly covered by a scarf and the sons with a hat in rasta colours (called a tam) which contains their dreadlocks. Strict Rastafarians neither cut nor comb their hair, which then twists naturally to form the dreadlocks.
▶ Sikh males do not have their hair cut and young boys have the hair plaited neatly around their head. When they are older, boys' hair is wound into a jura (a bun) contained by a small cloth covering and teenagers will eventually have a turban.

Health and hygiene

Good practice will be to talk with parents about your general approach to health and to understand fully any individual health needs of a child. In any emergency you should, of course, call the parent(s), at which point they will take over responsibility for their child. Some families will have specific concerns about treatment. Jehovah's Witnesses, for instance, are opposed to blood transfusions.

Your approach should also encourage children to learn good habits in hygiene. Some religious beliefs include a particular approach which should be respected. Muslim children, and some Sikhs and Hindus, are taught to use the right hand for eating and keep the left for dealing with personal hygiene. They are also shown important habits of handwashing before praying.

Celebrating festivals

Calendars and dates

The Western system of months and years is based on the movement of the sun (a solar calendar) and its origin is linked with a solar-based system of astrology. But many other parts of the world use a system based on the movements of the moon (a lunar calendar) and Far Eastern astrology is a lunar system.

The lunar calendar is shorter than the solar by about 11 days, so the dates of festivals based on a lunar calendar move in relation to the solar calendar. Festivals with which you are unfamiliar are not moving at random. You can get yearly festival calendars and leaflets from many of the suppliers listed at the end of this chapter and in the general list on page 193. Most religious festivals move from year to year, but their date is determined in a predictable way if you know the underlying system. Workers with a Christian background often express surprise at the changing dates, but this assumption arises only because Christmas is the same date each year. However, Easter is not a fixed date (see page 146).

Years

The tradition of dating used in Britain depends on taking a 0 for the year estimated for the birth of Jesus Christ and counting backwards from that point for years labelled BC (before Christ) and forwards for years labelled as AD (Anno Domini which is Latin for 'In the year of our Lord'). This system has continued, since it is well established within cultures influenced by Christianity, although more recent historical evidence suggests that Christ was probably born between 4–7 AD. The terms AD and BC are now tending to be replaced by CE (common era) and BCE (before common era).

Other faiths, and the cultures influenced by them, have different year dating systems. For instance, the Jewish calendar is counted from what is 3761 BCE in the Christian calendar, because that year is believed to be when the world was created. General information on festivals will give dates in the Christian European style calendar, but these will not necessarily be the same style or year as the calendar used by the given religious group.

How to celebrate festivals

Festivals are part of religious practice in most major world faiths. Celebrations will have religious meaning, although some festivals become part of cultural tradition and continue to be celebrated by families who are not very active within the faith. You can celebrate a number of festivals drawn from different world faiths. Such activities can be one way of helping children to become more aware of religions other than their own and of faiths that are not practised in their immediate community. Celebrating festivals can be a positive experience, but has to be organised with care if children are to learn with respect.

MAKE SOME CHOICES

You cannot celebrate all possible festivals and, if you tried, children and adults would become dazed and confused as one celebration followed another. You could celebrate the key festivals of the families whose children attend your setting and add a small selection of other festivals which will be a source of learning for everyone.

INVOLVE PARENTS AND THE LOCAL COMMUNITY

You can look beyond your immediate setting for support and information. Some of the children's parents, as well as local people, may be pleased to explain their faith and particular celebrations to you. Some may be happy to speak to the children in the setting or act as a guide in a visit to a local place of worship. Undoubtedly some early years, playwork and school settings will have a wider range of opportunities of this kind than others.

Be sure that you brief a parent, or local person, who speaks to the group or whom you invite to a school assembly. It is important that their approach is one of 'I believe . . .' or 'we believe that . . .' rather than 'what I am telling you is the only truth'. You need to exercise the same care in learning about religions as cultural traditions (see also page 81). Do not assume that the few people with whom you speak about a religion that is unfamiliar, have told you everything that there is to know.

RESPECT PARENTS' WISHES

Some parents will be open to your plans for their children to celebrate a wide range of festivals. But it is the parents' right to raise children within a given religion if they so wish. Some parents may be uneasy about celebrations other than in their own faith, although some may be reassured by your explanation that children are learning about a range of faiths. If parents feel strongly, then it cannot be good practice to insist. For instance, families who are Jehovah's Witnesses hold a Memorial Service on the day of Christ's death (a week before the Jewish Passover) but they do not celebrate Christmas, Easter, birthdays and a number of other celebrations because the main origins of these festivals are judged to be non-Christian.

Keep Festivals Separate

You should take a distinctive approach to each festival. Definitely do not explain one celebration in terms of the beliefs or events of a religion more familiar to you. Some festivals share a focus on light or the exchange of presents, but there will be differences as well as shared themes. So, do not describe Divali as 'a kind of Christmas' (or the other way around). And do not let it pass, if children make this comment. You might say that there are some similarities, but the two are different.

Show Equal Respect

The celebration of a range of festivals can encourage the children to respect the beliefs and traditions of others, but a great deal depends on how adults introduce and talk about the festival, and the underlying beliefs.

You need to avoid any implication that 'other people have colourful festivals' but 'we have serious religious events'. Unfamiliar celebrations, or those from faiths that are not represented in the group, should not be treated as exotic or 'just a bit of fun', in contrast to familiar festivals which are treated as normal and serious.

Consider how much time you spend on different celebrations. If you spend all of December on Christmas and only one or two days on any non-Christian festival, then your actions are saying as loudly as words that you value Christianity most highly. Celebrations in an early years setting should probably not last more than a few days for each festival. Young children lose the point of a celebration if it goes on for ever and the making of cards or other activities can become a chore. Many parents with over-excited young children would welcome less wind-up to Christmas in a nursery or pre-school setting.

Activities and Artefacts

Some of the festivals described in this section have activities that are a regular part of the celebration. There will be possibilities for creative work with the children.

▶ **You can make some choices about an activity. But do not feel that children have to produce something for every festival, nor that every child must make a card, lantern or drawing. You will lose the point of extending children's learning about a faith and a celebration, if the main message they gain is that they have to make a Hanukkah card before they can go back to play.**

▶ Celebrations with a long religious and cultural tradition should be respected in their own right and not just seen as handy source material for your early years or primary curriculum.

▶ Sometimes, a festival can be celebrated and explained to children through the support of a book recounting the main story of the festival, with pictures and conversation.

▶ Satisfying craft activities and enjoyable celebrations have a more serious meaning underneath. Explain to children in simple terms the reasons for making lanterns or cards. Be cautious about developing craft activities for religious traditions that are unfamiliar to you, since you could be disrespectful without intention. For instance, if you are a Christian, imagine how you might feel about a nursery that made a model of Jesus on the cross out of egg boxes and papier mâché.

▶ Many celebrations are linked with stories with a long history. When you recount, or read, such stories to the children be careful to treat all with equal respect. You should not, for instance, imply that the story of the Buddha is just a fairy tale whereas the Christmas nativity is an accurate historical account.

▶ Make sure that any activities with religious meaning are treated with respect. Children should never pretend to pray or do joke meditation or obeisance. If you work in a primary school, you may introduce children to some artefacts with religious meaning, for instance, the rosary used by Catholic Christians or the Seder plate used to celebrate Pesach (the Jewish Passover). Ensure the children realise that these are not play materials.

The following section outlines some important festivals with suggestions for celebrations in an early years setting.

Yuan Tan – Chinese New Year

Chinese culture has historically been influenced by Buddhism (see page 129), Confucianism (a system of social ethics established about 2500 years ago) and Taoism (a philosophical system of an equally long tradition). Reverence for family ancestors is also an important part of Chinese life. China is the source of the world's oldest lunar calendar and their years run on a twelve year cycle named after the animals, whom it is believed were the only creatures who answered the Buddha's call. For instance, 1998 is the year of the Ox (sometimes translated as Buffalo), 1999 of the Tiger and 2000 of the Rabbit (the Cat in some traditions). Chinese astrology is based on the year in which children are born.

The Chinese New Year falls within January or February and is celebrated with fireworks, giving sweets, flowers and other gifts. A substantial lion costume is supported by a number of dancers and the lion dance goes on throughout the day to the sound of drums and cymbals. The dragon procession is also popular because dragons are a symbol of good fortune. The Yuan Tan is a special time for children, who receive a red packet containing money to bring good fortune. The packets themselves (lai see) have messages of good fortune written on them.

The first full moon of the new year is celebrated with Teng Chieh, the Lantern Festival which will fall sometime in February. Many lanterns are made in various designs and strung out as decorations to welcome the longer days.

Possible Activities

▶ Talk about the celebration and read about what the New Year celebrations can mean to a family and to children.

▶ Make a lion mask or a dragon, either as a 3-D sculpture or a an effective dragon wall frieze.

▶ Make lai see with children and discuss what kind of good fortune you could wish each other for the coming year.

▶ Make lanterns out of paper and hang them in your setting. Talk about how the seasons revolve from longer days to longer nights and around once more.

Christmas

Christmas is a Christian festival marking the birth of Jesus Christ and held always on 25th December in the Western Christian church. The festival is held on the 6th January by the Orthodox church, which will be especially relevant if your setting includes Christian families who originated in countries such as Russia, Greece, Egypt or Serbia.

Christmas celebrates the arrival of the baby whom Christians believe to be the Son of God, who died on behalf of the sins of the world 33 years later at Easter. The giving of gifts between close friends and family is a reflection of the valuable gifts brought to Jesus and his earthly parents, Mary and Joseph, by three men (sometimes called 'kings' or 'wise men') who had travelled to see the child. Historical records suggest that Christ was probably born in January rather than December. But Christmas was fixed at the midwinter festival to replace pre-Christian festivities held at this time.

In Britain the Christian origins of Christmas have become muddled with cultural, rather than religious, traditions of Father Christmas, reindeer, cards, pantomime, decorated trees and the now relentless advertising pressures surrounding the traditional exchange of gifts. A simple approach to the festival may help children to distinguish the story at the centre of this celebration from all the commercial hype about the 'magic of Christmas'.

POSSIBLE ACTIVITIES

▶ Tell the story of Christmas through a book, cut out figures or a nativity scene.
▶ Make cards to give to friends and family. Explore images that are closely associated with the religious Christmas story: the star that led the three kings, aspects of the nativity scene, the angel who told Mary that she was to give birth or the candles that are lit in churches through Advent (the four weeks before Christmas) as a symbol of Christ as the Light of the World.
▶ Explore how children can make presents for friends and family. You might also talk about what they could give members of their family that are not tangible presents: some help over the Christmas season, patience with a younger sibling or affection for a mildly irritating older relative.

TO THINK ABOUT

If Christianity is the most familiar faith to you, you may find that exploring the important celebrations of other world religions brings a freshness to the original meaning of Christmas. I am not suggesting that your setting should remove all cultural, rather than religious symbols of the festival. But as your team plans for this celebration, why not discuss some element of a 'back to basics' approach. What are the key ideas and the main symbols of the real Christmas story?

For instance, you could consider **not** having someone dress up as Father Christmas. This cultural tradition started with a family member dressing up for the children. It is now a confusing situation in which children are likely to see Father Christmas figures in every large department store and more on the street with a charity collection tin.

Divali

This festival falls on a moonless night in late autumn (the exact date varies) and is celebrated by Hindus and Sikhs. For Hindus, the two main themes of Divali are:

▶ Reverence for the deva Lakshmi (also the wife of Vishnu), who is associated with wealth and good fortune and who is said to visit every Hindu home once a year. By the time Lakshmi visits, all family disagreements and any debts must be settled; the New Year then starts afresh.

▶ The story of Rama's rescue of Sita from the demon king Ravana. This story is only one part of the epic tale of the Ramayana.

Sikhs also celebrate Divali, but for them the celebration is associated with the release from Gwailor prison of Guru Har Gobind. The Sixth Guru refused to be released unless 52 Hindu princes were also given their freedom. To meet the Emperor Jehangir's demand, that only those who could hang onto the cloak of Guru Har Gobind could leave, he wore a cloak with very long tassels and all left safely.

During Divali, there are fireworks, cards are sent and gifts and food are exchanged. Oil lamps or candles are lit in the Mandir (Hindu) and Gurdwara (Sikh). Hindu homes are cleaned and tiled floors scrubbed ready for a Rangoli pattern to be drawn, which welcomes Lakshmi. Divali is a significant festival symbolising the triumph of light over darkness, knowledge over ignorance and good over evil.

A Rangoli pattern

POSSIBLE ACTIVITIES

▶ Talk about the festival and the idea of starting afresh in a New Year, not carrying on with quarrels.

▶ Read the story of Rama and Sita.

▶ Make diva lamps with the children. You do not have to light them if you are concerned about safety.

▶ Make cards – the illustrations are usually of Lakshmi seated in a lotus flower, Rama and Sita, or of diva lamps.

▶ Display Rangoli patterns or draw some that children can colour or decorate. Rangoli patterns are built around a central point and the patterns are often flowers with four petals or squares divided in symmetrical triangles (four is a significant number in Hinduism). The pattern is repeated in a shape that can finally be round or square and the repetitive quality represents the endless cycle of time.

▶ Make sweets or other foods that can be given. If you have a 'no sweets' policy in your setting you could consider relaxing the rules for special occasions.

Easter

This is a Christian festival which focuses on the death of Jesus Christ on Good Friday, which is a day of mourning and his resurrection three days later on Easter Sunday, which is a day of celebration. Good Friday is always the Friday following the first full moon of the spring equinox, which is one of the two points in the year when day and night are of equal length. Consequently, Easter is a variable date, falling within March or April. Any days of religious significance linked with Easter – like Shrove Tuesday and Lent – move accordingly.

In the Christian calendar, Easter is a more important celebration than Christmas because the faith revolves around the belief that Christ willingly died to take on the burden of the sins of the world. Some churches reduce or remove normal decorations for Good Friday, to show mourning for Christ's death and then churches are full of flowers on Easter Sunday to celebrate the resurrection.

Easter is associated with symbols of birth and renewal: flowers, eggs and young animals. Some of the activities have their roots in pre-Christian spring festivals. Rather like Christmas, you may need to help children find the religious significance of the celebration. Easter is increasingly buried in a welter of chocolate eggs, chicks and bunnies and an increasing commercial pressure to buy presents for children.

There are several important events in the weeks before Easter. Shrove Tuesday is just under six weeks before Easter. This festival is celebrated by feasts, dancing and dressing up in many countries. In Latin countries the day is known by the French phrase of *Mardi Gras*, which means 'Fat Tuesday'. Shrove Tuesday was the day that Christians traditionally finished off any perishable stores of dairy products and meat, so there would be no waste during Lent when diet was restricted by choice. Lent starts on the next day, Ash Wednesday, and runs to the Saturday of the Easter weekend. Lent covers a period of 40 days in which Christians remember the time that Christ spent in the wilderness before starting his years as a inspirational teacher. Shrove Tuesday in Britain has become traditionally Pancake Day.

POSSIBLE ACTIVITIES

▶ Talk about the Easter story and make the links to the birth of Christ celebrated at Christmas.

▶ Explore how the seasons can be linked to themes of death, rebirth and renewal. Easter is sometimes seen as a fresh start and new clothes or special costumes may be part of an Easter parade.

▶ Make pancakes on Shrove Tuesday and explain the background to this tradition. Perhaps talk about why people of different faiths sometimes choose to give up a food or to fast for a period of time.

▶ Hot cross buns used to be cooked and eaten only on Good Friday, with the symbol of the cross being a reminder of Christ's death. You could still cook or buy some buns, although they are now available all year round.

Hanukkah

At Hanukkah, Jews remember the recovery of the temple at Jerusalem after its destruction by Syrian invaders some 2000 years ago. When the Jews, led by Judas Maccabaeus, had cleaned the desecrated temple, they could only find enough purified oil to keep the lamp alight for one day. Yet, by a miracle, the small amount of oil lasted for eight days, until more oil had been purified. During Hanukkah, one candle of the Hanukiah, a nine-branched candlestick (sometimes called the Menorah), is lit each day, using the ninth candle (Shammash or Shammes) until all are alight.

During the eight days of the festival, which happens in December, Jewish people clean their homes and the synagogue. The Hanukiah is placed in the window of Jewish homes as a symbol of light, truth and goodness. Families celebrate together, with special foods, games and an exchange of cards.

POSSIBLE ACTIVITIES

▶ Buy or make some potato latkes. Butter biscuits are also popular for Hanukkah.

▶ Make Hanukkah cards, which can be illustrated with the image of the nine-branched candle or by the six-pointed Star of David.

▶ Children play the dreidel game during Hanukkah. A dreidel is a four-sided spinning top which is marked on each side with one Hebrew letter to give the message 'A great miracle happened here'. The Hebrew phrase is translated as Nes Gadol Hayah Sham. Players put equal quantities of nuts or sweets into the centre of a table and spin the dreidel. Depending on how it lands, the player takes nothing (N), half (H), all (G) or adds more to the pile (S).

Id-ul-Fitr

This festival is one of the times when Muslim families reaffirm their faith. The date varies from year to year. Id-ul-Fitr marks the end of Ramadan (see also page 137 about fasting) and is celebrated with special prayers, with visits to friends and family and a celebration meal. New clothes are often bought and children also receive presents of money and sweets.

If you work in an area with few if any Muslim families then you may celebrate only Id-ul-Fitr. But you should be aware that Muslims also celebrate the equally important Id-al-Adha. This event marks the willingness of the Prophet Ibrahim (Abraham of the Jewish Torah and Christian Old Testament) to sacrifice his son Isma'il for Allah, who intervened to stop the boy's death.

POSSIBLE ACTIVITIES

▶ Talk with the children about the festival and read a book about celebrating within the family.

▶ Make greetings cards. The patterns can be complex but must not feature any people or living creatures (according to the teachings of the Qur'an). You can use stylised flowers and abstract patterns.

▶ Show pictures of Mehndi patterns that Muslim women and girls use to decorate their hands on special occasions. Mehndi powder is designed to stain, so it can mark clothes and carpets and you may therefore want to avoid making actual patterns on children's hands.

Wesak

The most important event in the Buddhist year is a threefold celebration of the birth, enlightenment and death of the Buddha, all of which are believed to have occurred at the full moon the same month (also called Wesak) of different years. Zen Buddhists celebrate only the birth of the Buddha at this time.

Buddhists celebrate Wesak by decorating homes and shrines with flowers, candles and lanterns. There are street processions and offerings of food and flowers to the Buddha at the Vihara (place of worship). Buddhist monks receive gifts and special cards from children, who are given sweets in return.

Possible Activities

▶ Talk about the significance of the festival to Buddhist families.

▶ Although not associated only with Wesak, you could show the children examples of the detailed geometric mandalas that help Buddhists to focus and meditate.

▶ Talk with children about the exchange of gifts in festivals and the reasons why giving and receiving is so important in families.

Celebrating festivals

You will find that some of the main festivals in world faiths share some common themes, which you can explore with respect:

▶ Bringing light where there was darkness, light as a source of guidance or lighting the way to safety. Some festivals of light, such as Divali, also have their origins in hospitality to travellers.

▶ The struggle between good and evil as symbolised by people within traditional stories or the blend of good and bad in everyone.

▶ The New Year as a fresh start, a time to reflect on mistakes and to vow to improve, to resolve quarrels and start anew. Many festivals have the idea of renewal, symbolised by new clothes and cleaning homes.

▶ The significance of families and valuing children.

▶ Celebrating together, including a shared meal, which may have specific traditional foods. Giving thanks for food.

▶ The exchange of gifts, including food and sweets.

It can help children's understanding to alert them to shared concerns in different faiths, so long as the beliefs and festivals are not muddled.

There are obviously many more festivals that could be celebrated than are given in this section. Communities need and enjoy celebrations to bring people together. The books and materials listed on page 152 will give you other ideas.

TO THINK ABOUT

A careful celebration of festivals may be one strand in an attempt to counteract the impact of advertising on children and a view of celebrations as an excuse to make long 'want lists'. A focus on gifts is not exclusive to children in a Christian tradition. One afternoon, I listened with great interest as I walked home from school with my seven-year-old daughter and two of her friends. The conversation went along the lines of: 'What do you get for Christmas then?' Followed by, 'Well, what do your Mum and Dad give you for Divali?' There was a pause and then, 'Do you know how much money Hamid gets for Id?' This was followed by the answer and, 'He never does! That much!'

Children cannot be blamed for the excesses of a consumer-driven society. The African-American festival of Kwanzaa which started in the United States in the mid-1960s is now facing serious commercial pressures of cards, gifts and other products. Adults are responsible for trying to stem the tide as far as they can.

HALLOWEEN

Some festivals have a less obvious religious basis, unless you delve back for pagan origins. One example is Halloween.

Some nurseries or schools mark Halloween (31st October) with dressing up, pumpkins or craft activities. The American-style celebration which has increased in Britain over the last couple of decades actually owes much to the Irish tradition taken over by immigrants to the United States. There has also been a long tradition in Scotland that children dress up as Kelpies (ghosts) and wear masks to frighten away the witches. Some parents are not happy about the celebration of, what is at root, a pagan festival and some young children are frightened by talk of ghosts and witches. You might consider whether you celebrate Halloween and if so, how you explain the events to children. You should not dismiss parents' or children's concerns with 'it's just a bit of fun', anymore than you should with other festivals.

Visits

It may be possible to arrange visits to local places of worship, especially at times of the year that are especially significant for a particular faith. If you work in an area with a diverse population, you will be fortunate to have a wide choice. However, do not assume that children will necessarily attend the places of worship in your community. For instance, families in a mainly white area are not necessarily active Christians and the main beliefs and worship may be unknown to children.

Some possibilities follow:

▶ Buddhists worship in the Vihara. A Buddhist home will also have a shrine where family members can meditate in calmness on a daily basis.
▶ The Christian place of worship is given different names by different groups and it is respectful to ensure that you use the correct name. It may be church (Protestant or Catholic), chapel (Methodist or Baptist), meeting house (Quakers) or Kingdom Hall (Jehovah's Witnesses). Christians pray at home and some have a devotional area with holy pictures or a crucifix.
▶ A Hindu community will worship at the Mandir. Hindus will also pray and worship at home and many homes have a household shrine.
▶ Jewish families attend synagogue and pray daily at home. Orthodox synagogues seat males separately from females, whereas Reform groups have mixed congregations (and female Rabbis).
▶ Muslim men attend the Mosque. Women often pray at home, but can also attend the Mosque along with children.
▶ Sikhs attend the Gurdwara and some families also pray at home.

Different world faiths have their own places of worship

Respectful Behaviour on Visits

Find out about appropriate behaviour before you go and do not make the visit unless you, and the children, will follow normal behaviour for this place of worship. If possible, you can talk with parents who attend your setting and the place of worship. Follow up that conversation by contacting the relevant person within the faith (Vicar, Imam, Rabbi and so on).

▶ Explain to the children what will be expected of them – not total silence but peaceful behaviour. Explain your requests in terms of courtesy and respect for any place of worship. Warn children and their parents in advance about any requirements for dress.
▶ Some places of worship will ask that women and girls, and possibly also males, cover their head.
▶ Be ready to remove your shoes before entering the Vihara, Mandir, Gurdwara or Mosque.
▶ Many places of worship will request modest clothing for males and females, at least clothes that cover the upper legs and shoulders. This request may not be an issue in winter time, but summer clothing may need some forethought. Some places of worship may be less concerned about what the children wear than the adult workers.

Further resources

Materials

NES Arnold publish a range of festival packs appropriate to early years settings. The packs combine information with some suggestions for activities. (Address on page 194.)

The National Early Years Network (address on page 193) publishes a yearly wall chart with the major religious festivals.

Diaries produced by the major children's charities usually include the main celebrations for the year.

The weekly magazine *Nursery World* has seasonal features on festivals from different faiths.

The Pre-school Learning Alliance (address on page 194) has a series of illustrated *Festival Friezes*.

Religion in Evidence produces a wide range of materials. They are part of Technology Teaching Systems Ltd at Monk Road, Alfreton, Derbyshire DE55 7RL Tel 01773 830255.

Books

You need books that recount the main stories from world religions for children. A few examples are:

Stories From World Religions series published by Heinemann
Angela Woods (1990) *Faith stories for today* (BBC/Longman)
People of the Bible series published by Franklin Watts.

You also need some books that will bridge the gap between the sacred stories of different religions and what a faith means for a child and family day to day. Some possibilities are:

Our Culture and *My Belief* series published by Franklin Watts.
Bridges to Religion series published by Heinemann.

You also need background books that will provide you with information and ideas for activities within your setting:

Introducing Religions series published by Heinemann
Religious topics and *Seasonal festivals* series published by Wayland.
Fitzjohn, Sue, Weston, Minda and Large, Judy (1993) *Festivals Together – a guide to multi-cultural education* (Hawthorn Press)
School Curriculum and Assessment Authority (1994) *Religious Education – glossary of terms* (SCAA)
Walshe, John G and Warrier, Shrikala (1997) *Dates and Meanings of Religious and Other Festivals* (Foulsham Educational)
Some books written for older children and teenagers can be an excellent source of information for adults. A good example is the *Usborne Book of World Religions*

5

Good practice with disabled children

Terms

I have used the term **disabled children**, because it is the preferred phrase among disabled adults who share views about past and current experiences. The term is also widely used among professionals who work with disabled children and their families. But on this issue, as on any decision within any area of equal opportunities, you are not going to find everyone in full agreement.

The phrase **children with special needs** is still used, but the phrase brings some problems. All children have special needs in the sense that they have individual wishes, wants and specific needs at different times of their lives. The phrase was also originally supposed to cover children with very striking development, who could be described as gifted. But the words are almost always applied to disabled children.

The experience of disability

Disabled children in society

Into the 1980s, the dominant approach to disabled children and their families was to focus on the disability mainly in medical terms: diagnosis, treatment and management of the condition when, as often, no cure was possible. This has been called a **medical model** of disability. A re-evaluation of this approach has been stimulated by disabled adults sharing their memories and views of how they were treated as children. Parents of disabled children have also been vocal in their criticism of the medical model which treats their sons and daughters as a disability or a case, rather than as children. Some of the objections about lack of information, disrespect (to parents and children) and conflicting advice from different medical professionals are shared by families who do not have a disabled child, but have encountered poor practice from health and other services.

An alternative **social model** of disability has been promoted which focuses on the child as an individual. This model also highlights social conditions, outside the child's specific disability, that cause the child to be further disabled unnecessarily. The social model approach does not deny the value of appropriate treatments or medication, but stresses that children's life should not be driven by the disability label they are given or by a regime of treatment. Disabled children have individual needs, wants, interests and views about what happens to them, just like any other children.

Identifying and meeting children's needs

A couple of generations ago, disabled children were given a completely separate experience, often in residential accommodation. Carers often had low expectations for what children could manage and little respect for what they might want. The situation has changed in that parents have the legal right to seek mainstream provision, including schooling for their disabled child, supported by additional services appropriate to the child. Children with special learning, educational or health needs are affected mainly by three pieces of legislation:

- ▶ The Children Act 1989 – which mainly applies to social services.
- ▶ The National Health Service and Community Care Act 1990 – which covers the health service and related services in the local community.
- ▶ The Education Act 1996 – which relates to schools and related educational services and which replaced the 1993 Act without any substantial changes.

In their different ways, each of these laws requires that services and the relevant professionals should work in partnership with parents towards an assessment of individual children's needs and the provision of appropriate services.

Local education authorities (LEAs) have a duty to identify, assess, make and maintain a **statement** for children over two years of age, who are judged to need special education provision. A formal assessment has to be undertaken, involving the opinions of educational, medical or psychological services, and which takes into account parents' views. The whole process is supposed to be completed within a period of six months. A **Code of Practice** was established in 1995 which tightened up the whole procedure, including the need to have an **Individual Education Plan** (IEP) for each child in school who has a statement of special educational needs.

Children enjoy company

Provision available for younger disabled children can include different kinds of early years settings. Day nurseries, pre-schools and children's centres fall within the requirements of the Children Act 1989, which places an obligation on local authorities (the Social Services side) to provide for 'children in need', and disabled children are specifically included within this group. Nursery schools and classes come under the educational legislation.

The details of a child's individual statement should include:

1 The child's learning difficulties and how she or he functions in a detailed way, including strengths and weaknesses.
2 The child's specific learning needs, the kind of help that will be appropriate and how this input will help.
3 The facilities and resources that ideally should be made available to this child. (Decisions made by LEAs about what to offer have to weigh the usual problems of actual local resources and budgets against what is necessary or desirable.)

Each child's statement has to be reviewed every 12 months until she or he is between 12–14 years old, when a full reassessment must be undertaken.

As an early years worker or a playworker, you may be involved in different parts of the process:

▶ Good practice in your setting for observation and record keeping could make a positive contribution to a child's assessment. It is important that anything you contribute or write about a child is honest and descriptive. You need to give a well rounded picture of individual children. Describe what they can do and their strengths and not just a list of what they find difficult.

▶ If you are working in a school setting – nursery or reception stage – you may be involved in the development of a child's Individual Education Plan. Your LEA should have a standard form that has sections to cover the child's details as well as the learning plan with specific targets.

You will find more information about the law on children and disability from books and organisations listed from page 183.

THE INCLUSIVE APPROACH

This perspective on the care and education of disabled children stresses the value and possibilities of enabling children to remain within mainstream provision. There has been serious concern about the impact of dividing disabled children from their peers. But there are also misgivings about any overall policy that removes the option of special units or schools, where this service is in the best interests of children. You will find disagreement, as well as harmony, amongst professionals and parents who are active on behalf of disabled children.

There are certainly legitimate concerns about whether mainstream schools will have the facilities and are able to give appropriate personal attention to some children with specific disabilities. For instance, some parents of deaf children have been keen not to lose the advantages of special units. Parents have been very concerned about the impact on confused and anxious autistic children of the usual bustle of a nursery or primary group, unless there are enough adults to cope properly. Early years and school workers in their turn are very aware of the impact on a group of children of a young child with severe emotional and behavioural difficulties. There are no easy answers.

Yet there are definite advantages to all children of mixing together. Young children can be very straightforward about other children who are disabled. They want to know what is happening and require simple answers to reasonable questions. Experience of disabled friends can help to change society's images of disabled or very sick children. Children with physical disabilities may be bored and frustrated in a special unit with children who have severe learning disabilities. They want conversation, challenge, argument and play.

An inclusive approach is not some magical option and children will not benefit if positive opportunities are stressed, but limited attention is paid to practicalities. Proper assessment of the needs of the individual child is vital. What does the child need, who will deliver it and to what extent can her or his needs be met within your setting? The main issues in good practice are as follows:

▶ Disabled children should be seen and recognised as children, not seen only in relation to their disability or health condition.
▶ Specific needs that arise through a disability or health condition should be carefully assessed and met, as far as possible, through enabling disabled children to live, play and learn with other children. This approach does not propose that separate facilities should never be used, but that there should be a sound reason for proposing a different unit or school for a disabled child.
▶ Children should be able to see themselves in their early years, school or playwork setting. The play resources of the setting should reflect their existence and not create an image of the world in which no one is ever disabled or seriously ill.
▶ Neither the environment of the setting, nor the behaviour of workers or volunteers should lead children to be further disabled by what is offered, or not offered, and the way in which children's individual needs are met.
▶ Settings which currently have no disabled or seriously ill children should also consider what image of the world they are giving to the children who currently attend.

The wide range of disability

There are many different kinds of disability and the aim of this section is to give you a sense of the range. There is also great variation within any given diagnosed condition, so nobody is justified in comments like 'all children with cerebral palsy will . . .' or 'children with Down's syndrome will never . . .' You should also be aware that some parents wait some time for a firm diagnosis of their child's disability and for solid information on what is happening, why and how best to help their child. You will have to support the child as best you can, by focusing on their individual needs.

No worker, however experienced, could be expected to know about every kind of disability or illness. A realistic approach and good practice is to:

▶ Recognise the gaps in your knowledge or understanding.

▶ Be willing to find out, to listen and to learn: from parents, the children themselves, other professionals and the many organisations that are keen to inform and advise.

▶ Be ready to consider your expectations for disabled children and to assess your assumptions, some of which may be neither accurate nor helpful.

Some children are mainly or wholly physically disabled and the effect may be anything from mild to very severe. But some physical disabilities have associated learning difficulties. Some examples follow:

▶ Children with **spina bifida** share the condition that they have been born with some of the bones in their spine not properly joined together. The consequence is a split (*bifid* is from the Latin meaning 'split') through which the spinal cord protrudes. But there are different kinds of spina bifida. Some leave children with a slight swelling on the back, but with their physical and learning abilities intact. More severe versions can create paralysis, incontinence and additional learning disabilities.

▶ **Muscular dystrophy** is a progressive disease in which children's muscles waste away. There are variations of the condition but the form more commonly identified within early childhood is called Duchenne. Only boys are affected by Duchenne (but girls can have other forms of muscular dystrophy) and the condition is inherited. The young boy may be late in learning to walk and, as time passes, he has difficulties in physical coordination, finds it hard to get back up after a fall and has difficulty with everyday activities like climbing stairs. By late childhood, boys can have lost the ability to control their limbs and the muscle weakness can create poor posture, which in turn can make them vulnerable to chest infections.

▶ Children who are **blind** or **deaf** have a physical disability that affects the way in which they can learn in other areas of development, for instance, in how they use and develop their physical skills in a society that assumes children can see and hear.

▶ Children with **cerebral palsy** share a condition in which their brain fails to send the appropriate signals to their limbs. But there is a wide variation in this disability. Some children experience no more than mild difficulties in hand control. Other children have great difficulty in standing and moving their limbs in a planned, deliberate way. There may also be damage in other parts of the children's brain so that they may be deaf, blind and experience severe learning disabilities.

It is not always obvious whether a child has disabilities or a continuing health condition

▶ When a woman contracts rubella (German measles) in the first three months of her pregnancy, the result for her child can include deafness, blindness, cerebral palsy and severe learning disabilities. But the consequences of **rubella syndrome** are certainly not equally severe for all babies and children.

Children may largely experience learning disabilities and again the impact may range from mild to very severe. For example:

▶ Children's with **Down's syndrome** vary considerably in the impact of the condition on their learning. Children can have mild through to severe learning disabilities and some children have associated physical disabilities, for instance heart problems (which sometimes require surgery) or difficulties with hearing and vision. The experience of children with Down's syndrome and their families is a good example of how approaches and attitudes have changed. Two generations ago, it would have been regarded as wildly optimistic to propose that children with Down's would attend mainstream school and learn to read. Many children, who previously would have been placed in residential schools with minimal expectations for their progress, have shown what is possible with appropriate support.

▶ Children can have learning disabilities for a wide range of reasons, and there may not be a definite explanation and diagnosis. Children who show difficulties in their learning may have experienced brain damage during a protracted and difficult birth, as a result of accidental damage to the head in childhood or as a result of serious illnesses such as meningitis or whooping cough.

▶ Children with **autism** can have difficulties in learning to speak but their disability affects social communication in a broader way. Autistic children find it hard to learn and apply the social cues that are a natural part of everyday interaction with peers and adults. Autistic children can find the world a frightening and confusing place and many have behavioural difficulties.

▶ Learning disabilities such as **dyslexia** affect children's reading and writing. It is more severe for some children than others. Research into dyslexia has shown that children (more often boys than girls) may also have difficulties with physical coordination, with mathematical work (although some dyslexic children have no problems with maths) and managing sequences of activities.

Children may have variable or poor health as a direct result of their disability. Some children will have a continuing health condition that affects their choices and how they run their lives. Some examples are:

▶ **Cystic fibrosis** is a life-threatening condition that affects children's lungs and their digestive system. The mucus in their lungs is considerably thicker than it should be and blocks the bronchial tubes. Children have a persistent cough, difficulties in breathing and a vulnerability to chest infections. They need regular (sometimes daily) physiotherapy and swift treatment of infections. Cystic fibrosis also blocks the pancreatic gland which should produce the digestive juices that help the body to absorb fats and starch. Consequently, the child's body passes these nutrients straight through and the child fails to thrive. Children with cystic fibrosis vary considerably: some can manage more physical exercise than others and some need intensive physiotherapy. Children need to take medication to substitute for the working of the pancreatic gland and some also need to monitor their diet with care. Cystic fibrosis does not have associated learning disabilities; children's intellectual and communication abilities cover the whole range.

▶ Young children with **Down's syndrome** have a tendency to be more vulnerable to common infections like coughs and colds. The problem tends to lessen as the years pass and children's respiratory tracts grow larger. These may sound like very ordinary illnesses, but continued infections of this kind can affect a child's hearing, worsen existing hearing problems and affect a child's general well-being.

▶ **Asthma** is the most common chronic medical disorder in childhood, affecting an estimated 10% of children. Some children experience mild attacks of breathlessness, but about half of the group have more serious attacks with bad coughing fits and inability to get their breath. Some children have daily attacks and a serious asthmatic attack can be life-threatening.

▶ **Sickle cell disease** is an inherited blood disorder. The most common and severe form is sickle cell anaemia. Children are not ill all the time but can experience crises and are especially vulnerable to infections.

▶ **Diabetes** is an inherited condition in which the body is unable to use sugar and starch as energy. The pancreas fails to produce insulin with the consequence that the glucose, formed by the breakdown of sugars and starch, is not absorbed by the body and continues in the bloodstream to the kidneys in concentrations that are damaging. Childhood diabetes is called 'early onset diabetes' and children will have to be injected with insulin by an adult until they are old enough to take on this task for themselves. Children and also adults who are diabetic have to monitor their diet with care.

▶ **Epilepsy** is a consequence of an overload in the brain, when the normal and tiny electrical signals from groups of nerve cells become much stronger and overwhelm a nearby part of the brain. The result is a fit (major or minor) or a series of fits. Children and young people with epilepsy can continue with their lives and find ways to handle the likelihood of fits, including an explanation to close friends about what to do. However, some major fits have fatal consequences.

The range of causes

There are varied reasons for the different kinds of disability or health conditions.

CONGENITAL

Some conditions are described as congenital. This word means that the condition has been inherited by the child from their parents. There are different mechanisms for the passing on of genetically-linked conditions and, with some conditions, although there may be a genetic cause, inheritance is not the whole explanation. Environmental factors may contribute. Some examples of inherited conditions include: Down's syndrome, cystic fibrosis, haemophilia and muscular dystrophy. The genetic patterns can vary. For instance, the gene for the Duchenne version of muscular dystrophy can be carried and passed on by females, but the condition only shows itself in boys.

Some conditions have so far been statistically more frequent within some of the world's ethnic groups than others. Sickle cell anaemia, for instance, has been more common in families of African and Caribbean origin, and thalassaemia (a condition leading to an excess of iron in the body) in families of Mediterranean origin. But population movements and marriage between members of different ethnic groups has meant that both genes are likely to spread more widely.

EVENTS DURING PREGNANCY

Generally speaking, the foetus is very well protected in the womb, but some circumstances can cause lasting damage, with consequent physical or learning disabilities or poor health for the child. Some examples include: rubella caught during the first three months of pregnancy, prolonged and excessive drinking of alcohol (foetal alcohol syndrome), use of addictive drugs and HIV infection which crosses from the mother to the foetus.

TRAUMA AT BIRTH

Lack of oxygen at birth can happen for a number of different reasons and may cause brain damage in babies. The exact consequences will depend on how severe the brain damage and what parts of the brain are affected. Despite great advances in care, very premature babies can be at risk of later disability, as a result of the immature state of vital bodily organs when they are born.

ILLNESS AFTER BIRTH

Some serious childhood illnesses can have permanent consequences, even when the child has survived the illness itself. For instance, meningitis can leave children with hearing difficulties (the most common after effect), brain injury or epilepsy. Rheumatic fever can damage the heart, leading to formation of scar tissue, which in turn prevents the valves from opening and closing as they should.

ENVIRONMENTAL EFFECTS

There are few conclusive studies linking aspects of our environment to disabilities and health conditions. The claim that poor air quality is the main explanation for rising levels of asthma is not supported by studies in different countries. However difficult it is to prove, it is generally felt that the environment may play an important role in determining health and possible disabilities. Lead poisoning does have an impact on learning disabilities – problems can arise through children accidentally sucking on a lead-coated object or because they live close to very busy roads and intersections.

Early years settings need to consider ease of access for disabled children

ACCIDENTAL

Some children's physical or learning disabilities are the direct result of serious accidents, including those that involve damage to the head. Children may have accidents at home, when out at play and through being knocked down by traffic.

MULTIPLE POSSIBLE CAUSES

It is certainly not the case that each disability or health condition has a single, or obvious, cause. Cerebral palsy, for instance, can be inherited but this is rare. It can be caused by pre-natal events, for instance, rubella. But also a difficult and protracted birth, with oxygen deprivation, may lead to cerebral palsy and the condition is a risk of very premature birth. However, head injuries in serious childhood accidents can also lead to the development of cerebral palsy. For some children there may never be a credible explanation.

Partnership with parents

Parents and disability

Of necessity, many parents become relative experts on their child's disability or health condition. If you make time to talk with and listen to them, you will extend your knowledge in general and, importantly, you will understand far more about what the disability or health condition means for this individual child and family.

However, not all parents of disabled children are experts, or feel as if they are. Good practice will be to have conversations with parents in which you give time and pay attention, hoping to learn from them, but also sharing what you know. Show your willingness to support parents in finding out more, either about their own child's individual needs or about the condition in general. For instance, do not assume that parents will have heard about a relevant support organisation. Some parents manage with very little support or information from other professionals.

Your first contact with any individual parent should be a time when you are as concerned to hear about their child as you are to explain the way of working in your setting. Your conversations with parents of disabled children will cover many of the issues common to any first conversation. Some likely issues are:

▶ How best can you welcome children and help them to settle into the group? Ideally, of course, a parent will help to settle the child in, but how you can you support the process?

▶ Will it be sensible to prepare the existing group for the child's arrival? Perhaps a child's appearance or condition is likely to lead to comments and questions from other children. It is dishonest to pretend that there is nothing unusual about Katrin, if she is in a wheelchair and the first child with a visible physical disability to join your nursery. You could discuss briefly with Katrin's parent what you plan to say. You may wish to talk later with her parents about more general issues of how you answer children's questions in a respectful way.

▶ You need to know about children's individual needs. Even if you have previously worked with children with a particular condition, you still need to understand in enough detail how Rachel's epilepsy affects her, or the individual consequences of Michael's cerebral palsy.

▶ Approach the conversation with honesty, not pretending that the child is 'just like all the others' but avoid a focus on 'difficulties'. It is the difference between saying, 'What should I know about Patrick's diet?' and 'I suppose there'll be problems with food.'

▶ Find out if the child is taking regular medication and whether the setting will need to store and administer this if the child is young, or remind an older child to take his or her medicine.

▶ Are there particular health issues to which you need to be alert without being over-protective? Some children are vulnerable to any infections, some may be especially at risk from particular illnesses.

▶ For some disabilities and continuing health conditions, you must know what to do in an emergency, or how to recognise an emergency for a particular child.

▶ Be honest if you genuinely believe that the setting cannot meet a need. Be ready to ask and consult someone else or inquire about help from another professional, perhaps with physiotherapy.

It is important to be honest if you do not know what a child is likely to need, or if you do not understand what a parent has told you. Do not be uneasy about starting another conversation with, 'I don't think I'm really clear about . . .' It is far better that you struggle with potential embarrassment now, than that a child is put at risk because you were muddled.

All the relevant information must be passed on to any worker who may be involved with the child. For instance, it is of limited value that *you* can deal calmly with Rachel when she has a fit in the reception class, but the playground helpers have no idea what to do and panic when she has one during the lunch break.

It is possible that parents will not find out that their child has a specific disability until he or she has spent some time in an early years setting. Some parents may have been anxious for many months about their child's development or pattern of behaviour. They may have been told that their child will catch up, grow out of the problem or that there is nothing wrong and they are worrying unnecessarily. Such parents may be relieved that someone has listened to their concerns and that now perhaps they will receive some help. Alternatively, the parents may have been unaware of any problem and are shocked to be told that all is not well with their child. Your working relationship with parents will, of course, be different under these varied circumstances.

DISABLED ADULTS

Bear in mind that some parents will themselves be disabled. In some cases they will be the disabled parent of a disabled child, but not necessarily. Several issues may arise:

▶ It is as important that you build an individual relationship with this parent as with a child who is disabled. Parents whose children attend early years or school settings get used to be being known, at least partly, as 'Ricky's Mum' but will not appreciate being known as 'the one in the wheelchair'.

▶ Disabled parents may be pleased to share their knowledge and experience. But, as with any parent's special contribution, they may not appreciate being pigeonholed and the assumption made that disabled parents will not have expertise to offer on a broad range of issues and play activities.

▶ Avoid assumptions about what disabled parents could, or could not, offer. For instance, do not assume that Ricky's mother will not want to join a rota of parents who come in to support craft activities that need careful supervision. Perhaps you are thinking that may be too difficult with a wheelchair, when you should be making the invitation and then talking with her about any practical issues.

▶ Parents may have learning disabilities, rather than physical. The kind and extent of learning disabilities vary considerably, so it is impossible to make broad generalisations. But, for instance, you may be able to offer advice and support to Marie whose learning disabilities mean that she is uncertain how best to care for and play with her child. You may also be offering advice to parents who do not have learning disabilities but are uncertain of their parenting skills.

ACTIVITY

Consider one of the conditions mentioned so far and imagine that a child, with this disability or health condition, is soon to join your setting. Gather some general information about the condition. A good first step would be to contact the relevant specialist organisation (see the list on page 184).

Think over the following issues, and ideally discuss them with colleagues or fellow students:

▶ What do you need to know and understand in order to work well with this child? What can you do? Do not just make a negative list of what you can't do or problems.

▶ What questions should you be ready to ask the parent(s) and how can you put your queries in a positive way?

▶ Do you need to prepare the existing group for the child's arrival? What sort of questions might the children ask? Consider the actual words you could use to reply with honesty and respect.

▶ Imagine this child as a part of your group. Are there gaps in the equipment or play materials? Does this child's arrival make you think about the range of activities, how the setting is organised or the kinds of books that you have? (You will find more ideas from page 177.)

▶ Are there any points you should take up from this exercise, even if you do not currently have a child with this particular disability?

The parent group as a whole

Any setting has to find a suitable middle course between treating the presence of disabled or sick children as an issue about which other parents should be warned and taking an equally inappropriate stance of assuming that you shouldn't treat this particular child differently from any other – so parents don't need to know.

TALKING WITH PARENTS

If you have judged it sensible to prepare the children, then be ready for parents who ask questions because their children have shared information. Natasha might tell her mother, 'We're going to have Heena next week and she's blind.' Remember that the general body of parents will be no better informed than you were, before you learned about Winston and sickle cell anaemia for example. Their anxieties should be respected. Do not assume that parents are either making an unreasonable fuss, or that they are prejudiced against disabled children, unless their persistence or language genuinely suggests this conclusion. Be ready to answer factual questions. Parents might want to know if a condition is catching or whether you will still have enough attention for all the other children.

WRITING TO PARENTS

The presence of a disabled or sick child should not inevitably trigger a stream of letters home to all parents. However, there may be occasions when a letter is appropriate. For example:

▶ Perhaps a child, with severe behavioural or emotional difficulties, has had a prolonged outburst that distressed and frightened the other children. It would be appropriate to write under such circumstances, just as you may also need to consider whether your setting can genuinely meet this child's needs with your current resources.

▶ Some conditions are life-threatening and your group may experience the death of a child, whom you have all come to know and like. It would be appropriate to write to parents to inform them and to explain how you will deal with the children's questions and sense of loss. (See also page 181.)

FEELINGS ABOUT DISABILITY

Within the parent group, and your own staff group, there will be a broad variation in feelings, as well as knowledge, about disability and serious health conditions. There is a complete spectrum of appropriate reactions between the two extremes of sentimentality about disabled children and grim hopelessness. The wide range of emotions experienced by parents of disabled or very sick children can be better understood by reading some of the books suggested on page 177, as well, of course, by listening to parents who wish to talk.

Early years and playwork staff need to be prepared to deal with the feelings of members of staff or parents, who are themselves pregnant or whose partner is expecting a baby. If disabled children attend the setting, usual anxieties about the well-being of the baby can be heightened by an awareness of what can happen, however unlikely that is in terms of statistics. I became personally aware of this issue because I was working with the staff of a unit for severely disabled children while I was pregnant with my daughter. Workers and parents can care very much about individual disabled children and respect them, whilst not wishing for others to experience those children's frustration, and sometimes pain and distress.

Other professionals and organisations

In your setting you may have contact with other professionals who work with disabled children and their families. Be ready to learn from physiotherapists or speech therapists, so that you understand the work being done with children and can help where appropriate. However, it is important that talking with other professionals is not seen as more valuable than talking with children and their parents.

You may also find that you can be a support to parents who are trying to weigh up advice from different sources, some of which may be contradictory. The professionals involved with a family are supposed to work cooperatively, but some parents find themselves dealing with different sources of information, advice and firm views about how best to help the child. Some professionals are very useful and supportive. Others have a limited idea of ordinary life with a disabled child (or more than one disabled child) and the practicalities of juggling different priorities, including the needs of other siblings.

There is probably an organisation for every disability and serious health condition. Many organisations have a telephone helpline and publish informative leaflets or longer booklets. Some have local networks and support groups. On page 184 you will find a range of specific organisations and also some general organisations that would help you track down information and advice for particular needs.

Working well with children

Access in the centre

Contact with disabled children or parents can make you reassess ease of access to and movement around your setting.

▶ Many buildings have been modified to ease access by wheelchair or for anyone who has a physical disability that affects mobility. Generally speaking, improvements for disabled people are inclusive, that is, appropriate facilities can be used by anyone. For instance, sloped entrances rather than steps and more spacious toilets are an immense help to everyone who pushes young children in a buggy.

▶ How easy is it for anyone to move around your setting? Perhaps you take a considered look at how Michael, with cerebral palsy, will move around the room. It may dawn on you that creating more space for Michael will encourage you to remove some of the clutter that is unhelpful for the existing group, or that the narrow access to your book corner is the source of avoidable, minor collisions between children.

In many cases, you do not need specialist toys for disabled children

Building a relationship with children

Too many people, when they look at a disabled child, see the condition rather than the child. Good practice in early years, in playwork or schools is to develop a personal relationship with a disabled child as you should with any children who are your responsibility. Of course, you and your colleagues need to understand what the disability or health condition means for this child. But put this knowledge into practice in the context of working with individual children.

▶ You can have empathy, understanding and appreciation of children's frustrations. But avoid pity, either through sad looks or comments such as 'poor Winston' or 'brave little Heena'.

▶ Make sure that all the staff, including any volunteers or parent helpers, relate to children as individuals. It is more positive to explain to other adults that 'Michael has cerebral palsy' rather than use phrases like 'Michael suffers from cerebral palsy'. You are not pretending that cerebral palsy is a condition that anyone would chose to have. But the way you talk about Michael should leave nobody surprised that he has, for instance, an absorbing interest in dinosaurs and a wicked sense of humour.

▶ Children should never be described just by their disability or health condition, because this approach chips away at children's individuality. It is discourteous to say of children 'Freddy is our little Down's boy' or 'you know Rachel – the epileptic'.

Positive communication

Disabled children, young people and adults find far too often that thoughtless people assume any visible physical disability means that someone can neither communicate for themselves, nor understand what others say. Good practice is to ensure that you aim for full and courteous communication with disabled children, or with disabled parents or colleagues. You may need to guide volunteers in your setting or parent helpers towards good practice. You can also show the peers of a disabled child, through your actions or explanations, the importance of communication.

Means of Communication

Some children will have particular difficulties with communication – either for physical reasons or because of learning disabilities. Specific needs in communication should be addressed in line with what individual children need. For instance:

► Teja, who is deaf, will need children and adults to face her, so that she knows it is her who is being addressed, so she can see any signs and lip read, if possible. Children with slight hearing loss or variable hearing (for example, from glue ear) will benefit from the same attention. This approach is only an active extension of what is usual good practice in communicating with children. Young children, especially in a busy or noisy group, do not always realise that someone is talking to them, especially if their name is said at the end of the sentence, rather than at the beginning.

► Children who have physical difficulties in forming their words may need extra time and patience from an adult, or child, so that they can express their thoughts or ideas without feeling pressurised. Children with learning disabilities may take that bit longer than their peers to understand what has been said to them and to frame their reply.

► Children with physical disabilities, with or without additional learning disabilities, may need to communicate in ways other than words. Adults and peers have to be close and able to watch the child. Small gestures and sounds may communicate clear messages once you get to know a child.

► Some children may use, or be learning to use, sign language.

SIGN LANGUAGE

There are different sign language systems but in working with children you are most likely to encounter **Makaton**. This system was developed by taking a selected vocabulary from British Sign Language (BSL) which would be most useful to young children who were developing language. Makaton is carefully structured so that children first learn the signs for basic needs and more complex ideas are introduced step by step. The advantage is that children who take longer to learn language or who have severe learning disabilities can still gain a useful range of communicative signs.

Deaf children may use a combination of sign language, some spoken words and lip reading. At least one worker within the setting should learn to sign and hearing children are often enthusiastic to learn as well. Signing definitely does not mean that you stop talking – use both methods of communication. Some children with learning disabilities, for instance children with Down's syndrome, learn basic signs at the same time as learning to speak. A valuable description of one family's experience is given in Geoff Shaw-Champion's *Teaching Makaton to Chloe* (1990), available from the Down's Syndrome Association.

ACTIVITY

Disabled children who have limited spoken language often communicate in ways other than speech. If you have the opportunity, build up a written record of how one child communicates without words. You may be able to explore this activity if you are working with one or more disabled children. Alternatively, you may be able to talk with the parent of a disabled child. Explain carefully what you are doing and give the parent a copy of your written report. You might be looking at any of the following aspects:

▶ How does Louisa use sounds, perhaps a few words, facial expression or gesture to communicate?
▶ How does Tom show that he likes something – food, drink, or a game?
▶ How does Louisa show that she does not like something or wants to stop?
▶ What kinds of fun communication does Tom like – touch and tickling, making faces, blowing raspberries or sequence games like *Round and round the garden?*

Talking and Listening

Appropriate guidelines for communication with disabled children build on basic courtesy and add specific understanding about individual children. The discourtesies that enter adult communication with all children can be worsened by assumptions about disabled children. Rude or thoughtless adults tend to assume that children do not hear what is not said directly to them, that they fail to notice a dismissive body language of shrugs and gestures and that children are always interruptible.

▶ Talk directly with disabled children and ensure that the other children and parents do as well. Talk at a normal volume and dissuade any adult or child who raises their voice to a disabled child. Shouting does not make the words any clearer. In fact, raised voices can be intimidating and actually distort the words for a deaf child who hears only part, or is trying to lip read.
▶ Sometimes a child may be helped by a slower pace of communication, but not to the point where the words sound patronising. Shorter sentences and pauses to make sure that a child has understood, or to give space for a reply, are far better than long, droning monologues.
▶ Deal firmly, although courteously, with thoughtless comments that are made in front of but not involving a disabled child, for example, 'Does he understand?' or, 'Will she want a drink?' Your reply will depend on the circumstances but could include, 'Malcolm is deaf but he

understands well. Please talk directly to him so he can see your face.' Alternatively, 'I don't know if Ciara would like a drink. Why don't you ask her?'

▶ Any explanations that you give on the child's behalf should include her through your warm gaze. Perhaps the child cannot speak for herself, because she is still very young or her disability affects her speech.

▶ You can share practical hints with adults and other children, 'Tell Heena your name. She can't see you and she hasn't got used to the sound of your voice yet.'

Listen to children

So far, much of this chapter has concentrated on talking with and learning from adults. But children also develop into experts on how they, personally, feel about what has happened and will continue to happen to them. Some of the positive changes in attitudes to disabled children have arisen from the views of disabled adults, who have spoken about how they felt during childhood.

Regardless of the age of the disabled children with whom you work, there will be opportunities to learn from them. In a similar way, you should be open to opinions and feedback from all the children.

▶ You can learn a great deal by asking children what they would prefer and listening to what they tell you.

▶ Be ready to respond to children's full communication because sometimes their views will be expressed through facial expression, gestures or other bodily movements.

▶ Children can tell you, in different ways, about the kind of help they would appreciate and which actions are not actually helpful to them. It is important to listen to how children feel, and watch so they can show you. You need to ask questions such as, 'How would you like me to help?' Do not assume you know the best kind of assistance to give, if any.

Children whom adults describe as 'having special needs' do not necessarily feel 'special' in any positive sense. Some children may try to evade health routines that are important for their well-being, because it is more important in their eyes to appear to be like their peers. Time spent listening to children will help you to understand the troubles that are associated with disabilities or health issues that may seem minor to adults. For instance, children with eczema, even mild versions, can feel very self-conscious and have to deal with the other children's mistaken belief that eczema is a rash like chicken pox and so can be caught.

QUESTIONS ABOUT A CHILD

It is reasonable for children or adults to ask for information and, if necessary, your replies can gently correct a discourteous way of asking. 'What's wrong with her?' may be answered with, 'Joanne is having trouble breathing. She's using her inhaler.' 'Why does he dribble like a baby?' may be answered with, 'Michael has difficulty swallowing, but he's not a baby. He has what is called cerebral palsy.'

There is no need to make a curious child feel awkward with 'ssh' or 'it's not polite to look'. Their curiosity and questions are fine and you can guide them towards a courteous approach to their disabled peer. It may help to tell a child, or adult, the name of a child's disability. But also always be ready with an honest and simple explanation of what this disability or health condition means for everyday life. The parents of disabled children can often help you with sensible explanations; they have had plenty of experience. It is neither true nor helpful to say, 'Ciara is just like you' when this is obviously not the case. Straightforward explanations are best, for instance, 'The part of Michael's brain that sends messages to his muscles doesn't work properly. That's why he finds it hard to move where he wants.' Leaflets from the many specialist organisations (listed from page 184) are often a good source of simple answers to questions, from disabled children themselves or from their peers.

Play materials and games

People often think that disabled children will need specialist play materials and equipment. Some additional play materials may be useful, but much of your equipment will be suitable for disabled children. Many of the materials marketed for disabled children are enjoyable for all children. Soft play items and mats, soft construction pieces and ball pools were originally developed with disabled children in mind, but it swiftly became obvious that all children wanted a go.

▶ Disabled children enjoy the usual early years activities, such as sand and water play, as much as their peers. They will have a more enjoyable time with the company of other children and should not be restricted to 'special' equipment that either the other children are told to leave alone or that does not interest them. Some practical reorganisation may be needed to ensure that a child's wheelchair or standing frame can be placed close enough to an activity.

▶ Older disabled children should not be restricted to play materials that are clearly designed for much younger ones, perhaps on the grounds that they are safer or easier to handle. Children will understandably feel insulted if they are offered 'baby toys'.

▶ However, children with severe learning disabilities may not be ready to have play materials with very small parts, although you would usually make them available to a child of this age. You have to weigh up, with the help of the parents, whether four-year-old Annie is still likely to put small parts of a kit into her mouth. She will be stronger and her mouth will be bigger than a younger child's, so there could be a genuine risk. A child with severe learning disabilities may behave more like a younger child, for instance, still putting sand or plasticine in his or her mouth, and will need careful supervision.

▶ If children are spending some time learning a range of skills or understanding ideas, then you need a wide variety of play materials at the appropriate level. Children will get bored with a narrow range of books and toys.

Special programmes

Some disabled children will have special programmes of work, for instance: speech therapy, physiotherapy and directed physical exercises or a graded learning programme. Some children in your setting may have an Individual Education Programme (IEP) drawn up as part of their special educational needs assessment.

Any special work appropriate for individual children should be fitted into a full and rounded day or session. It is a question of balance in the life of children and their experience in your setting. Special work that will help a child's individual needs should be presented with care and shared enjoyment by the adult concerned. For instance, a child who is having physiotherapy as she lies across big coloured wedges may regard this as play, especially if these same wedges are generally used as play equipment at other times.

Disabled children can become unhappy and frustrated if they never seem to have a choice about what they do, or every activity is serious and adult-directed. Just like all other children, they need time to play. It is very important that disabled children should never be treated as if they are only the object of a special educational or physical programme. The children need and want enjoyable times, company, conversation and a chance just to mess about without any particular purpose.

Books

Without some care over the books that you offer to children, all of your group can develop an image of the world in which disabled or sick children (or young people and adults) are effectively invisible. There are definitely

Experiences and ideas can be shared through books

some good books available but you should not have to buy every one of them. Visit your local public library and put some friendly pressure on the librarian if the shelves have a noticeable lack in this area.

Broadly speaking, there are two kinds of books which are important in your approach to disabled children, regardless of the exact composition of your group:

1 Informative books written for children about specific disabilities or health conditions.
2 Stories that have disabled or sick children (or young people and adults) as main characters in the story.

The first kind of book is valuable because it gives straightforward information accompanied with illustrations of real children. Possibilities are:

▶ Nigel Snell's books in the *Events* series, published by Hamish Hamilton.
▶ The *One World* series, published by Franklin Watts, has a long list of titles, each beginning with *'I have . . .'* and covering a wide range of disabilities and illness.
▶ Organisations for disabled children and their families are a good source of information on books about a specific disability or health condition.

For instance, the Down's Syndrome Association book list includes several books suitable for explaining the condition to young children. One example is *Veronica's First Year* by Jean Sasso Rheingrover (published in 1996 by Albert Whitman).

Such books are useful for children to browse through in order to understand that disabled children have much in common with their peers as well as some differences or specific health needs. Certain titles can also be useful for a worker, or parent, who is supporting children in coming to terms with what their own disability means, and what it does not mean.

However, you will be giving an unbalanced view if disabled children are reflected only through their condition. Your setting also needs some books in which disabled children, young people or adults are active in the story, both as main characters or regular figures in the background. Disabled children are not always brave and happy, any more than their peers, nor do they always behave well. Some possibilities are:

▶ Emily Hearn's series about Franny who is in a wheelchair, for example, *Franny and the Music Girl* (1989). Some titles are published by Magi and some by the Women's Press.
▶ Sue Brearley's *Adventure Holiday* (A & C Black, 1991).
▶ Berniece Rabe (1988) *Where's Chimpy?* (Albert Whitman) – a book in which the main character has Down's syndrome.
▶ *Boots for a Bridesmaid* and *Are we There Yet?* by Verna Wilkins (1995) in which the child's parent is disabled (available from Tamarind, address on page 194).

ACTIVITY

Awareness about disabled children in fiction or featuring in general information books has lagged behind concern about the relative absence of children from minority ethnic groups. When disabled children are absent from books and play materials, how does that make them feel and what messages are being given to children as a whole?

▶ Look back at the discussion on page 99 on the presentation of minority ethnic adults and children in books and apply those ideas to the issues around disability and continuing health conditions.
▶ Look at the books in your setting, or browse along the shelves of your local book shop or the library. To what extent are disabled children or adults featured in books that are available locally?
▶ Take the activity on page 96 about 'Noky dolls' and, perhaps with a

colleague or fellow student, develop a similar example focusing on disability. For instance, if you are curly-haired, try to imagine that you cannot see yourself in any books except one about problems in hair care. This is the source of an insult – you have been called 'Frizzhead'.

Illustrations

All early years settings need a wide range of illustrations, from posters and murals to smaller postcards and material on an information board. There should be illustrations from some books, pictures of some of the jigsaws and other play materials.

▶ Can disabled children see themselves in some of these illustrations? Can they see disabled older children, young people or adults? Are they in recognisable everyday situations, not only specialist settings? Are the children in the posters or cards showing a variety of emotions: happy, excited, serious, absorbed, perhaps sometimes sad or thoughtful?

▶ Can all the children in your setting see their disabled peers? If you have no disabled children currently in your setting, then the illustrations may be children's main source of an image of disabled children.

▶ Take a careful look at any posters from charities where the main aim of the illustration is to encourage people to donate money. Organisations concerned directly with disabled or sick children and their families avoid stereotyped and pity-laden images in their general literature. But fundraising departments aim to pull at the heart strings and tend to emphasise problems and distress. Look back to page 95, where a similar issue was raised in connection with charity posters and children from minority ethnic groups.

Care and caring

Disabled children may need personal care and help from an adult at an age when many of their peers have learned to undertake most of their own basic self-care needs. Physically disabled children may be unable to manage some movements or to control bodily functions. Children with learning disabilities may take longer to understand and remember how to feed, dress themselves or manage in the bathroom. A positive and respectful approach to children's physical care is at the centre of good practice.

▶ Help offered to children should allow them to manage to the extent that they are able. Be ready to take the time that each individual child needs. Adults can learn how and in what way a child would welcome your help.

▶ Be encouraging and positive about what children can manage and acknowledge their frustrations with what they cannot do, or cannot yet manage.

▶ Encourage children to take care of their personal equipment: mobility aids, glasses, hearing aids. You are helping disabled children to learn the skills of self-reliance and responsibility that are appropriate for all children. Be aware that disabled children who regularly lose or break their equipment are not necessarily careless. Sometimes they are communicating their frustration or distress about their condition. You need to talk with and listen to the child and not focus only on the equipment itself.

▶ Depending on the child's disability, helpful adults will adjust how they offer support. For instance, a blind three-year-old girl will need a verbal description of what you are doing in dressing or helping her to eat a meal. She cannot see what you are doing, you need to tell her and guide her hands so she experiences through touch. A child with learning disabilities may need an activity like drinking or eating broken down into many tiny steps of learning.

▶ Some children will not have the bodily control for toilet training and will continue to wear pads or some kind of continence garment. The bathroom area used should offer these older children privacy and not look like a baby changing area. There is now a range of options for children to organise or control their continence and you should talk with their parents.

▶ Disabled children should have a key worker who attends to their intimate care needs. Children should be confident that only one, or at most two, people will help them in this way, so that care is offered within a close and respectful relationship. A system in which any worker may deal with a child's intimate needs can lead to disabled children believing that virtual strangers are allowed to touch them, and this increases the risk of later abuse.

▶ Be aware of your own physical well-being, in particular take care to protect your back when you lift or help a child to move, especially if he or she cannot help you much in supporting the weight.

Health needs

Disabled children may have related health needs that you need to understand. Children with continuing health conditions may have a vulnerability to infection or other specific needs. Knowledge will enable you to keep children safe without over-protecting them – sometimes a difficult balance to keep.

▶ Some children may be on regular medication, others may have medication that needs to be administered in an emergency. Make sure you understand what should be done and when. Bottles of medicine will be kept in a safe cupboard. But children's asthma inhalers must travel around the setting with them, especially in a large primary school. Some children have been put at risk by inappropriate rules.

▶ Some children may need regular physiotherapy to work their muscles. A physiotherapist may visit your setting, but sometimes it may be possible for a worker to learn appropriate exercises for a child.

▶ Some children may be generally vulnerable to infection or have specific health risks. For instance, Winston, who has sickle cell anaemia, will be vulnerable to infections and fevers and needs to be kept warm, especially in cold, damp weather. Because Patrick is diabetic, he needs a carefully balanced diet and regular meals, but he does not need special diabetic foods and he will not want to be made self-conscious at the meal table.

▶ Workers need to know important warning signs for a child. What, for instance, will happen to Winston if he has a sickle cell crisis? How should adults deal with Joanne's asthma attack? Under what circumstances should parents be called to the setting?

Some children's lives will be affected by a continuing health condition that means they need to exercise more care than most other children. Children may be ill considerably more often than their peers. Regular bouts of illness or time in hospital can be very wearing for children.

▶ Of course, there is the unpleasantness of feeling ill, sometimes very ill. Medication and necessary medical procedures may cause discomfort or pain.

▶ Children can also become bored and fed up, not only with being ill again but with the prospect of repeated illness stretching into the future.

▶ Being ill at home or experiencing repeated hospitalisations also disrupts children's friendships or makes it hard for them to make close friends in the first place.

▶ Illness interrupts the continuity of children's learning and their education when they start school. Families and workers can cooperate to minimise the disruptions, but they are still part of life for a child with a continuing health condition.

SERIOUS ILLNESS AND BEREAVEMENT

Some conditions are life-threatening and you may experience the loss of a child who has attended your setting. It is important to be honest with the other children in a group. Children become more upset and very confused when adults avoid talking about the death of someone known to them, or if adults actually lie.

▶ Tell the other children what has happened. They may need to be reassured that disabled children do not all die and that people can be very ill and recover. Answer any questions simply and honestly.

▶ Express your sadness at the loss of a child for whom you cared and let children express their feelings as far as they wish.

▶ Avoid saying to the children, or to the parents of the child who has died, that, 'Sasha's death was for the best. She is out of her suffering now.' This 'happy release' approach does not make parents feel better and can confuse children who know Sasha had a lot of pain and they still miss her very much, so who is happy in this situation?

▶ Be ready to talk about Sasha and more general feelings about loss as they arise. Leave her paintings on display and the photograph of the seaside trip when Sasha had such a good time. Do not immediately tidy away all these memories.

▶ Look for possibilities to support children in their understanding of loss and bereavement through books or other forms of play. But do not use books, or puppet play, instead of talking and listening when children want a conversation.

ACTIVITY

Adults often have difficulty in dealing with bereavement, especially when children are involved. Build up a file of information on two kinds of books:

▶ Informative books or leaflets for adults who are supporting children as well as dealing with their own sense of loss.

▶ Books specifically for children about serious illness, the death of a friend or relative.

You will find material by contacting Cruse-Bereavement Care and many of the organisations for different kinds of disability – addresses follow on page 184.

Discuss with colleagues or fellow students the main themes that emerge for a caring and honest discussion with children.

Further resources

Books

Alcott, Michael (1997) *An Introduction to Children with Special Educational Needs* (Hodder & Stoughton)
A basic introduction to the area with case studies.

Dare, Angela and O'Donovan, Margaret (1997) *Good Practice in Caring for Young Children with Special Needs* (Stanley Thornes)
A focus on daily practicalities of working well with young disabled children in early years settings. Information on the law and services.

Gatiss, Sheila and Russell, Philippa (1997) *Help Starts Here: a guide for parents of children with special needs* (National Children's Bureau)
Information about services and the legal situation for children and their families.

Jeffree, Dorothy and Cheseldine, Sally (1984) *Let's Join In* (Souvenir Press)
Ideas for play and leisure with disabled older children.

Jeffree, Dorothy and McConkey, Roy (1993) *Let Me Play* (Souvenir Press)
Ideas for play with young disabled children.

Kerr, Susan (1993) *Your Child with Special Needs* (Hodder and Stoughton)
Advice and information that is as useful to early years workers as to parents.

Lansdown, Richard (1980) *More Than Sympathy: the everyday needs of sick and handicapped children and their families* (Tavistock)
Informative and understanding about the reality of life for disabled children, or those with continuing health conditions, and their families.

Lansdown, Richard (1996) *Children in Hospital: a guide for families and carers* (Oxford University Press)
A practical account of good practice in hospital care and the impact on children and families of continuing health conditions.

Mason, Micheline (1993) *Inclusion, The Way Forward: a guide to integration for young disabled children* (National Early Years Network Starting Points No. 15)
Looks at the process of integrating disabled children and the underlying values of the system of education and care.

Pre-school Learning Alliance (1997) *Children with Special Needs in Pre-schools* (Pre-school Learning Alliance)
Practical advice about children in early years settings.

Slater, Mary (1993) *Health For All Our Children: achieving appropriate health care for black and minority ethnic children* (Action for Sick Children – address on page 184)
Practical issues that arise with children from different ethnic backgrounds.

Organisations

I have listed organisations relevant to conditions mentioned in the chapter. Please use the general organisations and suggested books for information about conditions which are not covered. All organisations offer information and advice, some operate a telephone helpline and many have a mail order publications list. Some have support groups and local networks, others also undertake or fund research. I have only given an explanation of an organisation when its title is not self-explanatory.

ACT, 65 St Michael's Hill, Bristol BS2 8DZ Tel: 01272 221556
> This organisation is the Association for Children with Life-threatening or Terminal Conditions and their Families.

Action for Sick Children, Argyle House, 29–31 Euston Road, London NW1 2SD Tel: 0171 833 2041
> Publications, information and advice for families whose children are spending time in hospital.

Advisory Centre for Education (ACE), 1b Aberdeen Studios, 22–24 Highbury Grove, London N5 2DQ Tel: 0171 354 8321
> Advice and information on the state education system. They publish the detailed guide *Special Education Handbook* (1996).

Association for Spina Bifida and Hydrocephalus (ASBAH) Asbah House, 42 Park Road, Peterborough, PE1 2UQ Tel: 01733 555988

British Diabetic Association, 10 Queen Anne Street, London W1M 0BD Tel: 0171 323 1531

British Dyslexia Association, 98 London Road, Reading RG1 5AU Tel: 01734 668271

British Epilepsy Association, Anstey House, 40 Hanover Square, Leeds LS3 1BE Tel: 01532 439393

Centre for Studies on Inclusive Education, 1 Redland Close, Elm Lane, Redland, Bristol BS6 6UE Tel: 0117 923 8450

Council for Disabled Children, 8 Wakley Street, London EC1V 7QE Tel: 0171 843 6061
> Publications and research projects on disabled children and young people.

Cruse-Bereavement Care, 126 Sheen Road, Richmond, Surrey TW9 1UR Tel: 0181 940 4818

Cystic Fibrosis Research Trust, Alexandra House, 5 Blyth Road, Bromley, Kent BR1 3RS Tel: 0181 464 7211

Down's Syndrome Association, 155 Mitcham Road, London SW17 9PG Tel: 0181 682 4001

Handicapped Adventure Playground Association (HAPA), Pryor's Bank, Bishop's
Park, London SW6 3LA Tel: 0171 731 1435
A focus on adventure play, and playgrounds, for disabled children.
They publish the journal *Let's Play* and a range of posters.
MENCAP, 123 Golden Lane, London EC1Y 0RT Tel: 0171 454 0454
Information and advice on a wide range of learning disabilities.
Muscular Dystrophy Group, Nattrass House, 7–11 Prescott Place, London
SW4 6BS Tel: 0171 720 8055
National Asthma Campaign, Providence House, Providence Place, London
N1 0NT Tel: 0171 226 2260
NDCS (National Deaf Children's Society), 15 Dufferin Street, London EC1Y
8PD Tel: 0171 250 0123
Planet (Play Leisure Advice Network) c/o Save the Children, Cambridge House,
Cambridge Grove, London W6 0LE Tel: 0181 741 4119
Offers information on play and leisure for disabled children, young
people and adults.
Royal National Institute for the Blind (RNIB), 224 Great Portland Street,
London W1N 6AA Tel: 0171 388 1266
Advice and information on all aspects of blindness.
Scope, 12 Park Crescent, London W1N 4EQ Tel: 0171 636 5020
An organisation concerned with all aspects of life with cerebral palsy.
Sense (National deaf-blind and rubella association), 311 Gray's Inn Road,
London WC1X 8PT Tel: 0171 278 1000
Supports families with children who have multiple disabilities.
Sickle Cell Society, 54 Station Road, London NW10 4UA Tel: 0181 961
7795
Thalassaemia Society, 107 Nightingale Lane, London N8 7QY Tel: 0181 348
0437

6

Overview

Key issues in good practice

Your role in a child's life

Raising children is a long-term project in which workers have an important short-term role to play during early childhood. Your responsibility is to create as positive an environment as possible for the period of time that you are responsible for individual children. For some children you will enhance the supportive work that their parents have done and will continue to do. For other children you will help them to see other possibilities, about themselves, other people or the world at large. You cannot control children's later experiences or negative influences outside your setting, but you can ensure that children's time with you is as positive as possible.

In a positive atmosphere, children will make many friends

Knowledge and understanding

Of course, you cannot know everything. You are not expected to be an expert on all major world faiths or on the wide range of disabilities that can affect children. But good practice is to be willing to recognise the gaps in your knowledge, to find out information when necessary and to unravel confusions that you do not understand. Your sources can be various:

▶ People you know, including colleagues, parents and other family members of children who attend your setting and other professionals with whom you have contact. Also, the children themselves.

▶ Relevant organisations who often have advice lines, reading lists and suggestions for other organisations or suppliers of books and materials.

▶ Books, booklets and leaflets, articles in journals and magazines.

▶ Television programmes – look ahead for useful programmes at times when you do not normally watch and record them.

▶ Do not generalise too widely from one source of information. Keep an open mind and be ready to continue learning.

Communication

You will learn a great deal through conversation with others. The important issue is, of course, to listen as well as talk.

▶ Talking with other adults will extend your knowledge but also will give you some insight into views different from your own. Sometimes it will be helpful to discuss another perspective, perhaps you will realise that you have overlooked an aspect of your work. At other times, you may continue to disagree, but you will understand more about why someone does not share your point of view.

▶ Talking with children will help you to understand how they grasp the issues and to what extent they understand what you are talking about. If you listen and, equally important, watch the children, you will be able to gauge when they have had enough of talking. Always be aware of children's reactions, whether you are sharing knowledge or explaining why you do not want them to use offensive words to each other, for example.

▶ If you show parents, colleagues and children your respect, then you are far more likely to receive their respect.

A constructive view of mistakes

Good practice with children is to behave in such a way that they can learn from their mistakes. You also need to establish good practice in how you judge your own behaviour and that of colleagues and parents. Adults feel no better than children do when they are given no room for error.

▶ Sometimes you will react to a child, colleague or parent in a way that was based on lack of knowledge or thought. If it is appropriate, then apologise and think about, or find out, how you could react more constructively in the future.

▶ Good practice benefits from reflection, both thinking over events and issues yourself and in conversation with colleagues, and often parents or children as well.

▶ Do not be unreasonably hard on yourself; you will not get it right first time all the time. Work towards a confident approach with colleagues who understand why it is important to have the freedom to make mistakes.

▶ A team needs to create an atmosphere in which everyone can offer a positive challenge that helps adults or children to reconsider. Pushing people onto the defensive is not good practice and can lead to a more entrenched set of attitudes and behaviour.

▶ You are not responsible for everything that happened in the past, but you do share a responsibility for the present and the future for children and how society develops.

In what kind of world do you want her to grow up?

► You will not please everyone. Like most other areas of practice, groups and individuals are not always in agreement over aspects of equal opportunities.

Reflect and review

Good practice does not stand still, but you do not change what you do just for the sake of novelty. It is important to consider what you do and why. Informal conversation with colleagues or team meetings can support careful reflection on your overall approach to the children, to parents and how you organise your setting. Teams have to ask themselves not only 'what are we aiming to do?' but also 'what do we actually do day by day?' How thoroughly are equal opportunities principles really put into practice; do policies on paper really become observable actions?

Good practice includes a willingness to look from perspectives other than your own. You are not expected to deny your own sources of personal identity. But it is appropriate that early years, playwork and school workers make the effort to understand unfamiliar beliefs or ways of life. You need to be ready to explain your own perspective to others – what you do and why. Do not assume that the basis for your practice must be obvious. It is good practice to be willing to explore the beliefs and assumptions that you bring to your own practice.

One step at a time

In working with children, your aim is to lay positive and firm foundations. You are not trying to complete the whole building. You are not, for instance, trying to help children to learn everything about early science within the relatively short time they are with you. You can reasonably hope to share some learning, stimulate an interest and develop an open attitude to learning. These hopes apply across all the different areas of equal opportunities. You are trying to open doors for children, to extend their understanding, encourage them to seek out further information or possibilities about how to treat other people.

Good practice in equal opportunities is supported by knowledge and understanding, but it also has to be underpinned by awareness. You should notice the children, in all their individual variation. Listen to the children as well as talk with them. Be aware of yourself: your assumptions, actions and conversations. Be ready to learn, to reflect and to adjust. You will then provide a positive role model and children will learn from you.

Further resources

The following books, and the organisations and suppliers, address the broad framework of equal opportunities. You will also find suggestions at the end of each chapter which relate specifically to a particular area.

Books

Brown, Babette (1996) *All Our Children: a guide for those who care* (BBC Publications)
> Practical ways of promoting equal opportunities.

Children's Rights Development Unit (1994) *Report 12: Children and violent conflict: Northern Ireland* in *UK Agenda for Children* (CRDU)
> Description of the impact of the situation in Northern Ireland on a generation of children. Linked with the UN Convention on the Rights of the Child.

Derman Sparks, Louise (1989) *Anti-Bias Curriculum: tools for empowering young children* (National Association for the Education of Young Children)
> Information and practical ideas for overcoming barriers based on race, sex or ability. Available from Community Insight (address on page 193) and the National Early Years Network (address on page 193).

Dixon, Bob (1990) *Playing Them False: a study of children's toys, games and puzzles* (Trentham Books)
> Discussion of the ideas and values that are communicated to children through their play materials.

Dunant, Sarah (ed) (1994) *The War of the Words: the political correctness debate* (Virago)
> Collection of essays taking different perspectives on words and actions within equal opportunities.

Garrett, Helen and Taylor, Judith (1993) *How to Design and Deliver Equal Opportunities Training* (Kogan Page)
> A useful book if, as a senior worker, you are planning in-house workshops or generally exploring how your team can learn in this area.

Hughes, Bob (1998) *Games Not Names – the training pack* (Playboard)
   A practical approach through playwork for the experience of children
   in Northern Ireland.
Millam, Rosalind (1996) *Anti-Discriminatory Practice – a guide for workers in
   child care and education* (Cassell)
   Information and practical suggestions for equal opportunities on ethnic
   group and religion.
Pre-school Learning Alliance (1996) *Equal Chances: eliminating discrimination
   and ensuring equality in playgroups* (PLA)
   Explains the importance of an active approach, with plenty of practical
   suggestions.
Save the Children (1991) *Playing in Harmony – an early years resource pack*
   (Save the Children – Scotland)
   Information and ideas of general value but also appropriate to the
   particular ethnic group variation in Scotland.
Slaby, Ronald, Roedell, Wendy, Arezzo, Diana and Hendrix, Kate (1995)
   Early Violence Prevention: tools for teachers of young children (National
   Association for the Education of Young Children)
   Practical strategies to support cooperation in early years settings and to
   show children an alternative to aggressive approaches. Available from
   the National Early Years Network (see address on page 193).
White, Peter (1995) *Playing Fair: a guide to tackling discrimination* (National
   Early Years Network/Save the Children)
   Practical advice about being honest with children and encouraging
   respect of other people.
Various authors (1995) *The Co-ordinate collection on equal opportunities*
   (National Early Years Network)
   A collection of key articles, updated, on many aspects of equal
   opportunities that have been published in *Co-ordinate*.

Magazines

You will often find practical articles in magazines and journals. I find the
following publications especially helpful:

▶ *Nursery World* and their occasional supplement *Nursery Equipment*
▶ The National Early Years Network journal *Co-ordinate*
▶ The National Children's Bureau journal *Children UK*
▶ *Child Education* is also worth checking for useful features.

Organisations

The following organisations could be helpful for any of the areas within equal opportunities covered within the book. You may want to track down other organisations not listed here or at the end of any of the chapters. Try the national directory, *Organisations concerned with young children and their families*, available from the National Children's Bureau or National Early Years Network (published in 1995, but update sheets are also produced).

Advisory Centre for Education (ACE), 1b Aberdeen Studios, 22-24 Highbury Grove, London N5 2EA Tel: publications 0171 354 8318, advice line (2-5 pm) 0171 354 8321
A source of information and advice about education in state schools.

Children's Legal Centre, University of Essex, Wivenhoe Park, Colchester, Essex CO4 3SQ Tel: 01206 873820
Publications and information about the legal position of children on a wide range of issues.

Community Education Development Centre (CEDC), Woodway Park School, Wigston Road, Coventry CV2 2RH Tel: 01203 655700
Projects and publications in the broad area of community education. Practical resources and photo packs.

Development Education Centre, 998 Bristol Road, Selly Oak, Birmingham B29 6LE Tel: 0121 472 3255
Booklets and photo packs on different aspects of development education, families around the world and varied cultures.

Early Childhood Unit, 8 Wakley Street, London EC1V 7QE Tel: 0171 843 6064
Consultancy, training and information in the field of early childhood and parenting. The Unit is part of the *National Children's Bureau* which publishes books, reading lists, the journal *Children UK* and the *Highlight* series.

Early Education (known in full as the *British Association for Early Childhood Education*), 111 City View House, 463 Bethnal Green Road, London E2 9QY Tel: 0171 739 7594
Promotes good practice in early years work. Offers advice and information. Publications, conferences and the journal *Early Education*.

Equality Learning Centre, 365 Holloway Road, London N7 6PA Tel: 0171 700 8127
Resource and information centre for anyone working with under-eights. Publications and workshops, reading and resources lists, posters.

National Coalition Building Institute, PO Box 411, Leicester NE4 8Z1 Tel: 0116 2603232

Runs workshops for adults to explore the roots of negative attitudes and build a positive approach. A central value is that there is no 'hierarchy of oppression'; everyone's hurt counts.

National Early Years Network (NEYN), 77 Holloway Road, London N7 8JZ. Tel: 0171 607 9573

Publications, including the *Starting Points* series, the journal *Co-ordinate*, some posters. NEYN also has an annual programme of training courses.

Pre-school Learning Alliance (PLA), National Centre, 69 Kings Cross Road, London WC1X 9LL Tel: 0171 833 0991

Promotes quality care and education for under-fives. Many early years groups are affiliated to the PLA and most are now known as pre-schools rather than playgroups. Publications and posters are available from PPA Promotion, 45-49 Union Road, Croydon CR0 2XU Tel: 0181 684 9542

Save the Children, 17 Grove Lane, London SE5 8RD Tel: 0171 703 5400

Publications and research projects concerned with services and policy for children. Booklets, photo packs and other visual materials.

Working Group Against Racism in Children's Resources, 460 Wandsworth Road, London SW8 3LX Tel: 0171 627 4594

Publish a useful booklet *Guidelines for the evaluation and selection of toys and other resources for children*. This review also lists some suppliers.

Mail order

The organisations listed offer resources that address more than one area relevant to equal opportunities.

Bangladesh Resource and Multi-cultural Book Centre, 1ˢᵗ Floor, 23-25 Hessel Street, London E1 2LR Tel: 0171 488 4243

Mail order and a centre that welcomes visitors. A wide range of books, photos, dolls and puppets, dressing-up clothes and crafts.

Christian Aid, PO Box 100, London SE1 7RT Tel: 0171 620 4444

Ask for their education catalogue.

Community Insight, The Pembroke Centre, Cheney Manor, Swindon SN2 2PQ Tel: 01793 512612

Mail order company specialising in publications about children and a range of books for children. Community Insight also run workshops.

Galt Pre-School, Culvert Street, Oldham, Lancashire OL4 2GE Tel: 0161 627 5086

A wide range of play materials and equipment.

Harmony Publishing, 14 Silverston Way, Stanmore, Middlesex HA4 4HR Tel: 0181 954 2541

Dual language storybooks and cassettes.

Letterbox Library, Unit 2D, Leroy House, 436 Essex Road, London N1 3QP
Tel: 0171 226 1633
Mail order children's books, specialising in a non-sexist and
multicultural lists. Dual language books and posters.

Magi Publications, 22 Manchester Street, London W1M 5PG Tel: 0171 486
0925
Publish children's books in different languages and some dual language
books.

Mantra Publishing, 5 Alexandra Grove, London N12 8NU Tel: 0181 445
5123
A wide range of books in different languages, tape and story packs, and
song collections.

Multilingual Matters, Frankfurt Lodge, Clevedon Hall, Victoria Street,
Clevedon, Avon BS21 7SJ Tel: 01275 876519
Books and journals about bilingualism.

NES Arnold Ltd, Ludlow Hill Road, West Bridgford, Nottingham, NG2
6HD Tel: 0115 971 7700
Dressing-up clothes, dolls reflecting different ethnic groups, dolls with
visible disabilities, posters and display cards and other play materials.

Pre-school Learning Alliance through *PPA Promotion*, 45–49 Union Road,
Croydon CR0 2XU Tel: 0181 684 9542
For booklets and a set of festival friezes.

Oxfam Trading, PO Box 72, Bicester, Oxon OX6 7LT Tel: 01865 245011
A source of cards, crafts, and artefacts from around the world.

Save the Children, 17 Grove Lane, London SE5 8RD Tel: 0171 703 5400
Booklets and posters. Ask for their education catalogue.

Tamarind Ltd, PO Box 296, Camberley, Surrey GU15 1QW Tel: 01276
683979
A wide range of books, puzzles and posters that show children of
different ethnic backgrounds and disabled children and books with
non-sexist themes.

Unicef, 55-56 Lincoln's Inn Fields, London WC2A 3NB Tel: 0171 405 5592
A source of pictures of children around the world – in postcard sets or
diaries. Some jigsaws and games from a wide range of national sources,
music tapes.

Links to child care courses

This book will support your study in the following courses.

▶ NVQ/SVQs in Early Years Care and Education, levels 2 and 3.
▶ NVQ/SVQs in Playwork (levels 2 and 3).

These sets of occupational standards do not have separate equal opportunities units. Good practice in this area is an integral part of many of the units at levels 2 and 3. The proposed content of the book would support many of the explanatory statements within the units. Chapter 5 supports unit C17 in the level 3 NVQ/SVQs in Early Years Care and Education.

Modules on equal opportunities and anti-discriminatory practice in the CACHE training programmes:

▶ Module 1 in the Certificate in Child Care and Education.
▶ Modules C and R in the Diploma in Nursery Nursing.
▶ Modules 5 and 13 in the Advanced Diploma in Child Care and Education.

The book will also support the content on equal opportunities in the core modules on *Practices in Child Care* (1040L) and *Professional Practice* (1044L) in the BTEC National (nursery nursing) in Childhood Studies.

Index